Danielle Olivia
Mengue Me Nkoulou

Spiritual
Warfare

Scripture quotations are taken from the following translations:

New International Version (NIV)
Holy Bible, New International Version®
Copyright © 1973, 1978, 1984, 2011 by Biblica, Inc.™
Used by permission. All rights reserved worldwide.

New King James Version (NKJV)
Scripture quotations taken from the New King James Version®.
Copyright © 1982 by Thomas Nelson. Used by permission.

Amplified Bible (AMP)
Scripture quotations taken from the Amplified® Bible.
Copyright © 2015 by The Lockman Foundation.
Used by permission.

Disclaimer
This book is written for spiritual, educational, and theological purposes. It does not replace personal study of Scripture, prayer, pastoral counsel, or professional care. The author encourages readers to seek God directly and to test all teaching by the Word of God.

References to psychological concepts, belief systems, or cognitive frameworks—including, but not limited to, cognitive behavioral principles—are included for illustrative and educational purposes only. They are not intended as clinical instruction, diagnosis, or mental health treatment, nor do they replace the guidance of licensed medical or mental health professionals.

Publishing Information
Published by: Danielle Olivia Mengue Me Nkoulou
United States of America

ISBN: 979-8-9944451-0-5

Introduction

Beloved Brothers and Sisters, I welcome you to a journey unlike any other—one rooted in the power of testimony and transformation. My name is Danielle Olivia Mengue Me Nkoulou. I am a minister of the Gospel and a lover of Jesus' heart. From a young age, I was exposed to the demonic realm. I learned to recognize its patterns and processes. I was initiated into witchcraft (The Bwiti) and faced countless attacks in my childhood. Yet, this is not where my story makes the greatest impact.

The most impressive part, however, is not what I have gone through, but what I have overcome. To reach victory, I first had to be rescued—saved, restored, reborn, rebuked, processed, redeemed, rebuilt, and loved. Jesus saved me and taught me how to recognize Him, trust Him, surrender to Him, process with Him, and stand in His victory.

With this foundation, I invite you into the heart of my message: learning to stand in the victory of Jesus by refusing to be ignorant of the devil's schemes. It may surprise you that I never intended to write a book, especially not on spiritual warfare. Originally, I thought I would release a musical album before ever writing. Yet now, it is truly an honor to answer the call and use my gift to equip the Body that I love so much.

My journey continued as I spent time with God, letting devotion turn into teaching. Despite my broken English, I was led to preach. When these teachings grew too long, I framed them into a book. I pray that, as you read, you will be inspired to pause and turn to your Bible.

This book is not the answer. I am not the answer. Jesus is the answer. I am simply a witness, sharing my revelation from the foundation God has given me. I pray this book accelerates your deliverance because:

"They overcame him by the blood of the Lamb, and by the word of their testimony."-Revelation 12:11

Let that be our agreement.

Table of Contents

Section I

Introduction to Spiritual Warfare

Chapter 1 — What is Spiritual Warfare?

What Is Spiritual Warfare?

I think it is important to start this book by answering this question. We can all answer it in theory, or in part, and sometimes that is the problem. Fragmented information can be harmful when misused.

When we hear the term *spiritual warfare*, we mostly picture humanity fighting against darkness. We think about the tools we use to fight evil spirits, such as prayer and fasting. All my life, I have heard people say, "Prayer and fasting is spiritual warfare." Another common idea is the study of demonology, but that sometimes leads to two extremes.

One extreme is the glorification of Satan's power over us. The other is an unholy obsession with all things supernatural and mystical.

Both extremes have created fear in the Body of Christ and obsession outside of the Body. Because of that fear, many now reject the truth that was meant to bring clarity and knowledge to this subject.

Spiritual warfare is a truth that is necessary to navigate and establish the victory of Jesus. It is knowing how to put on the armor of God. It is the revelation that the armor of God is not something you remove, but something you become. It is sound doctrine—something that equips the mature believer in the areas of defense, standing, and resisting the adversary of our souls.

Spiritual warfare is covering yourself with the Blood of Jesus, recognizing that the voice of His Blood speaks the Word of God.

Spiritual warfare is not just prayer and fasting; it is comprehending *why* we pray and fast. It is a curriculum that God needs you to learn so that you can be fully successful in your Christian experience.

Chapter 2 — The meaning and etymology of Spiritual Warfare

The term "Spiritual Warfare" is formed from two words: *spiritual* and *warfare*. To grasp its meaning, each must be examined on its own before its combined significance is considered.

Spiritual — Etymology and Definition

The word *spiritual* carries meaning across multiple languages. In Latin, *spiritus* refers to breath, wind, soul, or life force. The suffix *-ual* means "relating to" or "belonging to." In the Hebrew Scriptures, *ruach* (רוּחַ) signifies breath, wind, or spirit. In the Greek New Testament, *pneuma* (πνεῦμα) also means breath, wind, or spirit, while *pneumatikos* (πνευματικός) describes what pertains to the spirit, what is of the unseen order.

With this background, when something is described as spiritual, it is not imaginary. It is unseen yet real. It originates beyond the physical and produces effects within it. This may appear as events, encounters, or recurring patterns that stem from the invisible and manifest in daily life.

Warfare — Etymology and Definition

The word "warfare" also holds layered significance. In Old French, it means war, battle, or conflict. In Old English, *faran*, from which *fare* is derived, means to journey, to move forward, or to advance. In Hebrew, *milchamah* (מִלְחָמָה) refers to war, combat, or active fighting. In Greek, *strateia* (στρατεία) describes a military campaign, an organized conflict carried out with planning and purpose. Warfare, then, is more than opposition. It involves preparation, movement, and deliberate confrontation.

When these meanings are brought together, "Spiritual Warfare" refers to organized resistance and engagement that originates beyond the physical world.

The order of the words matters. The conflict described is not natural in origin, nor is it approached with natural means. It is rooted in the unseen and must be addressed through principles that align with that dimension.

The domain of the spirit belongs to God alone, and only He reveals the pattern required for this kind of conflict. If warfare involves preparation and execution, and spiritual refers to what is invisible, then spiritual warfare becomes the act of standing and advancing according to divine instruction.

Knowledge of tools or awareness of opposition, by itself, is insufficient. Success in this area requires submission to God's direction, His timing, and His process.

"For the weapons of our warfare are not carnal, but mighty through God to the pulling down of strongholds." (2 Corinthians 10:4)

Chapter 3 — What Does The Bible Say About Spiritual Warfare?

Spiritual warfare is part of sound doctrine. Sound doctrine is not a single idea; it is a framework of kingdom truth that functions as a system supported by spiritual laws and divine principles that believers must learn, accept, and live out. That is why it cannot be reduced to fighting demons alone. It is also about walking within God's order so that His victory becomes your position, not just your hope.

To grasp what Scripture teaches about spiritual warfare, we must first examine where the concept is introduced and how it unfolds. The Bible interprets itself. When an idea first appears in Scripture, the person through whom it is revealed carries the original revelation given by the Holy Spirit. That first mention establishes the foundation of the concept. When the foundation is clear, there is no space for distortion, abstraction, or personal commentary.

Spend time with God long enough for Him to reveal the full picture, not a sketch. A sketch invites personal colors shaped by preference, trauma, or history. A finished painting carries God's intention. When he completes the picture, truth no longer depends on interpretation; it transforms the one who beholds it.

The second framework is observing how spiritual warfare is demonstrated throughout Scripture. From Genesis to Revelation, God's people engage in conflicts that are not resolved by physical weapons, but by faith, obedience, prayer, and divine instruction.

These moments reveal how God teaches His people to stand, resist, and overcome through His strategies.

We study spiritual warfare this way because every truth must be submitted to God's revelation. When God reveals a picture, that picture becomes the foundation. I refer to this as the *integrity of a thing*—the discovery of what something truly is through God's perspective, not man's interpretation.

When we immerse ourselves in discovering and uncovering the "integrity of a thing," we discover:

Identity / Name → what it is by design, not what people call it. It is an inherent truth from the Creator. In Genesis 1, God names things according to their nature and origin.

Purpose (Function / Assignment) → why it exists, its reason for being, as intended by God. The Bible teaches that everything God created has a purpose. Genesis 1:11 says that when God created heaven and earth, He charged the earth to bring forth grass, herbs, and seed. According to God's voice, as He calls you, He gives you a command to exist, and that command is your function.

Order (Wholeness / Goodness / Divine Order) → how it is meant to be used or expressed according to the order God established, resulting in goodness and harmony.

Wholeness / Soundness → biblical integrity implies an internal consistency where one's beliefs, character, and actions are in harmony with God's Word (Proverbs 11:3). There is no hypocrisy or being "two-faced."

Order → it refers to adhering to the divine order God established, doing what is right and just (Proverbs 21:3).

Goodness → when a thing is used as intended and in the right order, it produces good fruit or outcomes, reflecting God's original creation, which He declared *"very good"* (Genesis 1).

The first direct mention of the concept using the actual word "warfare" in a spiritual context is in the New Testament:

"For though we walk in the flesh, we are not waging war according to the flesh. For the weapons of our warfare are not of the flesh but have divine power to destroy strongholds." (2 Corinthians 10:3–4)

This does not mean the idea of spiritual warfare did not exist before, only that the term appears explicitly here. The principle of spiritual warfare is found throughout Scripture. The concept begins as early as Genesis 3, when the serpent tempted Eve, and continues throughout:

Exodus (deliverance through obedience and divine intervention).
Daniel (angelic warfare in the unseen realm).
The Gospels (Jesus casting out demons, resisting temptation).
Ephesians 6 (the armor of God).
Revelation (final cosmic battle between light and darkness).

In 2 Corinthians 10:3–4, Apostle Paul says,

"For though we walk in the flesh [as mortal men], we are not carrying on our spiritual warfare according to the flesh and using the weapons of man. The weapons of our warfare are not physical [weapons of flesh and blood]. Our weapons are divinely powerful for the destruction of fortresses."

In this passage, Apostle Paul makes it clear: we walk in the flesh, but we do not carry on our warfare in the flesh. Our battle is not carnal. We cannot use natural weapons to win it. It is a spiritual war, and it must be engaged using spiritual weapons.

These spiritual weapons are so powerful that they pull down strongholds, break generational curses, and tear down spiritual fortresses. When you engage in spiritual warfare the right way, using the right tools, you do not just win for yourself—you win for generations to come.

Let us look at some examples of spiritual battles in the Bible, where people used God-given weapons to defeat the enemy.

Exodus 7–12 — Moses vs. Pharaoh

Weapon: Prophetic decrees and signs. Moses did not fight Pharaoh with a sword, but with miracles, instructions from God, and obedience.

Exodus 17 — Battle with Amalek

Weapon: Intercession. Moses's hands lifted in prayer decided the battle. When his hands were up, Israel won. When they dropped, Israel lost. This was spiritual warfare through prayer posture.

Joshua 6 — The Fall of Jericho

Weapon: Worship and prophetic obedience. The walls fell because the people marched, blew trumpets, and shouted, following God's instructions.

Judges 7 — Gideon's Army

Weapon: Obedience and prophetic action. Gideon won with 300 men using torches, trumpets, and jars. It was about God's strategy, not man's strength.

1 Samuel 17 — David and Goliath

Weapon: Faith in covenant and prophetic declaration. David spoke of victory before the fight because he knew God's covenant promise. He defeated Goliath by faith and prophetic boldness.

2 Kings 6 — Elisha and the Invisible Army

Weapon: Prayer for spiritual vision. Elisha prayed for his servant to see in the spirit: *"Those who are with us are more than those who are with them"* (2 Kings 6:16).

Daniel 10 — Angelic Warfare
Weapon: Fasting and prayer. Daniel's prayers triggered war in the heavens between angels and demonic princes.

Matthew 4 / Luke 4 — Jesus vs. Satan in the Wilderness
Weapon: The Word of God ("It is written"). Jesus defeated Satan by quoting Scripture, not with physical force.

Mark 5 — The Legion of Demons
Weapon: Spiritual authority. Jesus commanded demons to leave using His spoken word.

Acts 16 — Paul and Silas in Prison
Weapon: Praise and worship. Their worship caused an earthquake and opened prison doors.

Now that we have laid the foundation of what spiritual warfare is —its definition, its place in Scripture, and its biblical examples—we can move forward.

Section II

Good vs Evil: The mandate of perception

Chapter 1 — The Remedy

I've taught on this topic many times—through teaching, Sunday sermons, and master classes. The name of my counseling ministry was revealed to me through the revelation of this concept. I am convinced this revelation is a fundamental reset to keep you in the "now" of God through all seasons. I believe every believer should know and pursue this. It is central to how we nourish, protect, and build a Christian foundation. This is not a one-time event, but a daily formula for life. I've seen this topic bring deliverance to people and help those searching for God to discover Him.

We can spend days describing evil from our own perspectives or from the perspective of world events. Some definitions may seem correct, but first, we must understand that God is our center. Truth belongs to Him. Our definitions and perceptions must be governed by Him alone.

Today, evil has become subjective. We often mislabel evil as good and good as evil. This distortion clouds our connection to God's reality and prevents us from fully entering His kingdom. Without addressing this gap, we risk basing our concepts on emotion and perception rather than on truth, leading to partial understanding and widespread spiritual confusion.

This is heresy: a biblical idea formed outside of God's truth. Heresies are ancient, present from the beginning. Today, broken doctrines create incomplete believers—what the Bible calls stiff-necked.

I am not going to lie—this evil software, a term I use to describe the mental system or way of thinking that calls evil good and good evil, is pretty clever. Satan definitely studied for this one. What amazes me the most is the progression of that lie over time: from the deception and subjection of a wrong idea, to its acceptance and execution, and finally to its establishment and multiplication. But not only that—we see that wrong idea, that lie, being replaced by what is presented as real truth. It is visible in people's lives and behavior.

But what is the remedy? The remedy is a simple, universal practice that breaks the power of deceptive thinking. However, despite its simplicity and universality, it is often neglected. Instead of remaining in God's presence, where He can reveal things in us that could instantly heal us, we tend to spend more time seeking false prophecies. The remedy is the renewing of your mind in the Lord.

Renewing your mind is the remedy for many devilish schemes—especially the system of "calling good evil and evil good." It is both a remedy and a Christian mandate. Practicing it brings instant alignment with God. It requires discipline and continually connects you to God's truth. It is a spiritual workout that uproots generational lies and patterns the enemy built.

Paul expresses and explains this concept—this remedy, this mandate. Your mind is not simply getting new ideas or new perceptions; it is more than that. It is about reconnecting yourself to the integrity of any idea by submitting it and researching it in the hands of the One who has created all ideas. The soul, the mind, and the body need this to function, to grow, to be set free, to stay in the light, and to remain in perfect alignment with the will of God.

Let's look at Romans 12:2 and see how we learn to apply this remedy and why.

Romans 12:2

New International Version (NIV):

"Do not conform to the pattern of this world, but be transformed by the renewing of your mind. Then you will be able to test and approve what God's will is—His good, pleasing, and perfect will."

New King James Version (NKJV):

"And do not be conformed to this world, but be transformed by the renewing of your mind, that you may prove what that good and acceptable and perfect will of God is."

Amplified Bible (AMP):

"And do not be conformed to this world [any longer with its superficial values and customs], but be transformed and progressively changed [as you mature spiritually] by the renewing of your mind [focusing on godly values and ethical attitudes], so that you may prove [for yourselves] what the will of God is, that which is good and acceptable and perfect [in His plan and purpose for you]."

There are four key principles we learn from this verse. First, there is a pattern, conformity, value system, and philosophy attached to this world. Here, "pattern" refers to the repeated style or design of thinking and acting shaped by the world's influences. The word pattern comes from the Greek word *suschēmatizesthe (syschēmatizesthe)*, meaning to conform to, to follow, or to take the outward shape of something. In Hebrew thought, the closest root idea is associated with the words *tabnît* or *tsurah*. *Tabnît* is used in Exodus 25:9 to describe the pattern, model, form, or blueprint of the tabernacle. *Tsurah* is used to describe the shape, form, figure, or appearance of something.

Second, God does not want us to subscribe, conform, live, be reformed, take on the shape, design, receive the blueprint, or be molded by it any longer—and there is a reason why.

Third, transformation happens through the renewing of your mind. To renew your mind is to replace the world's perspective with God's, to exchange old patterns for His truth. When you adopt His way of seeing, thinking, and responding, you are reshaped from the inside out and brought into spiritual maturity.

Fourth, you must be able to test, approve, and recognize for yourself the perfect will of God. You cannot recognize true good if you do not know what God calls good. Without God's standard, you cannot truly know evil. Without renewing your mind, you will not recognize God's will or truly know Him and His plan for you.

This application is a gift; it is for your good. It is possible that what you have been calling good may not actually be good according to God, and what you have been calling evil may not actually be evil according to God. If you do not make renewing your mind a practice, your perception will remain shaped by the world.

When applied continually, spiritual warfare becomes falling in love with the application and the discipline produced through renewing your mind in the Lord. It becomes a lifestyle so deep that your revelation of anything is always birthed in integrity.

Chapter 2 — Realignment

When we hear "good," we rarely think of God; instead, we think of ourselves. We see beauty, comfort, and what pleases us, linking good to personal desire. But what we call good constantly shifts with moods, cravings, and worldly standards. Society teaches us to chase what looks successful or desirable. Even gratitude is filtered by what the world values. Eve called the forbidden fruit good before she tasted it—because she desired it.

When we seek pleasure, comfort, approval, or beauty, we often chase ourselves rather than God. Rather than worship what is right, we worship what feels right and call it "*good.*" However, true good does not always shine or bring comfort. Instead, it can cause pain or present a challenge. Yet God's good is eternal, unchanging, and life-giving.

This chapter is about realigning with God's definition of good and evil. Before that, we must recognize the faulty foundation we have accepted—not entirely our fault, but one we are responsible for correcting. We must examine, question, and measure what we call good against God's standard.

Let's look at some worldly synonyms of "*good,*" pointing to self rather than God:

Attractive — Pleasing to the senses; valued for appearance rather than spiritual integrity.

Beautiful — Inspires admiration or desire; appeals to personal taste, not necessarily to God's heart.

Successful — Achieving goals or recognition; measured by human standards, not divine approval.

Popular — Liked or approved by others; dependent on human judgment, not eternal truth.

Trendy — Following fads or cultural norms; fleeting and shaped by society, not by God.

Entertaining — Provides enjoyment or distraction; serves the flesh or ego rather than spiritual growth.

Comfortable — Produces ease or relief; avoids challenge rather than cultivating obedience to God.

Desirable — Coveted or craved; focused on personal pleasure, not godly purpose.

Luxurious — Indulgent or lavish; appeals to ego or status, not humility or spiritual discipline.

Pleasurable — Gives satisfaction or delight; rooted in self-gratification, not obedience to God.

High Status — Confers social importance; valued for human recognition, not godly honor.

Rich / Wealthy — Possessing abundance; points to worldly security, not spiritual blessing.

Powerful — Control over others or circumstances; emphasizes dominance, not service to God.

Impressive — Evokes admiration; appeals to pride rather than godly integrity.

Famous — Known or celebrated; valued for human attention, not divine purpose.

Well-liked — Approved or appreciated by people; often compromises truth to gain acceptance.

Tolerant (modern, permissive) — Accepting without discernment; prioritizes comfort over conviction.

Convenient — Easy or accessible; chosen for personal ease rather than a divine calling.

Safe — Free from risk or danger; chosen to protect self, not to follow God's direction.

Fun — Provides enjoyment or amusement; satisfies fleeting desire, not spiritual depth.

All these things point to self—our desires, comfort, or status—and not to God. They are reflections of the flesh, society's programming, and worldly perception. They are not inherently wrong, but if they are the only measure of what you call *"good,"* then they are incomplete and, in that sense, misguided.

When we think of *"evil,"* we often imagine things that are against us—things that take away what we love, what we desire, or what brings us comfort. Our perspective is limited. We see evil as anything that slows us down, blocks our progress, or prevents us from getting what we want. Good is often seen as getting what we desire quickly; evil is anything that delays it, even if the delay is for our own good. We think of evil as ugliness, discomfort, or anything unappealing.

Yet, just as our understanding of *"good"* is shaped by the world, so is our perception of evil. Society teaches us to fear certain behaviors, ideas, or people, and we inherit these judgments without questioning them. What the world calls evil is often simply inconvenient, uncomfortable, or different from our personal taste. I am not saying that there is no a visible, systematic system of evil in this world. I am stating that our measurement is sometimes wrong, because human preference cannot be the standard measurement of what evil is.

If God were only what we wanted Him to be, then anything that challenged our desires would appear evil. But if an obstacle exists for our growth, correction, or God's purpose, can it truly be called evil?

So many things are often labeled *"evil"* because they challenge personal comfort, convenience, or preference—not because they are inherently opposed to God. True evil, as God defines it, is rebellion against Him, disobedience to His will, and the corruption of the heart.

I have spoken about the renewal of the mind before, but I want you to see how this revelation builds layers within your Christian experience. The renewal of the mind is closely connected to the act of carrying our cross. Jesus said, *"Whoever wants to be my disciple must deny themselves and take up their cross daily and follow me"* (Luke 9:23). To deny oneself is to die to distorted definitions, inherited values, and worldly measurements. It is the daily discipline of laying down what feels right in order to walk in what is true.

The renewal of the mind is also how we love the Lord with our minds. Jesus said, *"Love the Lord your God with all your heart, with all your soul, and with all your mind"* (Matthew 22:37). Scripture reveals how our love is to be expressed toward God, and that response has to be obedience. As John 14:15 says, *"If you [really] love Me, you will keep and obey My commandments."* Loving Him means following and keeping His commands. To love the Lord with yourself is to follow the prescription Scripture gives for each part of who you are. When it comes to the mind, one of those instructions is found in Romans 12:2. When you practice the discipline of renewing your mind, you are loving the Lord with your mind, which is true mental health.

Lastly, you cannot follow Jesus while thinking like the world. His path requires a transformation of both heart and mind. First John 2:15 warns,

"Do not love the world or the things in the world. If anyone loves the world, the love of the Father is not in him. For all that is in the world—the cravings of sinful man, the lust of his eyes, and the boasting of what he has and does—does not come from the Father but from the world."

To follow Jesus, we must reject worldly patterns and allow God to renew our thoughts.

Chapter 3 — Discovering What Is Evil

Anything that is not pleasing to God is evil. Evil did not begin on Earth; it began with pride and rebellion in the spiritual realm. The first act of evil in creation was Lucifer's fall, as Isaiah 14:12–15 makes clear. The prophet describes a being who sought to elevate himself above God, declaring his own will in opposition to the Creator's authority.

New International Version (NIV):

"How you have fallen from heaven, morning star, son of the dawn! ... You said in your heart, 'I will ascend to the heavens; I will raise my throne above the stars of God... I will make myself like the Most High.' But you are brought down to the realm of the dead, to the depths of the pit."

New King James Version (NKJV):

"How you have fallen from heaven, O Lucifer, son of the morning! ... For you have said in your heart: 'I will ascend into heaven, I will exalt my throne above the stars of God... I will be like the Most High.' Yet you shall be brought down to Sheol, to the lowest depths of the Pit."

Amplified Bible (AMP):

"How you have fallen from heaven, O star of the morning [light-bringer], son of the dawn! ... But you said in your heart, 'I will ascend to heaven; I will raise my throne above the stars of God... I will make myself like the Most High.' But [in fact] you will be brought down to Sheol, to the remote recesses of the pit."

From this passage, we see that the origin of evil is pride—the desire to elevate the self above God. Pride produces self-centeredness, selfish ambition, and rebellion. Lucifer's five "I will" statements expose the heart of evil:

"I will ascend into heaven."
"I will exalt my throne above the stars of God."
"I will sit on the mount of the congregation."
"I will ascend above the heights of the clouds."
"I will be like the Most High."

Evil is not an abstract concept. Its substance is iniquity. Iniquity gives evil form and presence. It exists internally, within the heart, mind, and desires, and externally through actions. Internal iniquity takes root first, shaping what we love, desire, and pursue.

Scripture explains this clearly. First John 2:15–17 describes how worldly desire flows from this internal condition:

"For all that is in the world—the lust and sensual craving of the flesh, the lust and longing of the eyes, and the boastful pride of life—do not come from the Father, but are from the world."

What begins internally does not remain hidden. Internal iniquity eventually produces external works of the flesh. Galatians 5:18–22 shows this progression:

"Now the practices of the sinful nature are clearly evident... sexual immorality, impurity, sensuality; idolatry, sorcery, hostility, strife, jealousy, fits of anger, disputes, dissensions, factions; envy, drunkenness, riotous behavior, and other things like these. I warn you, just as I warned you before, that those who practice such things will not inherit the kingdom of God."

Evil can be summarized in two forms: internal iniquity and external works of the flesh.

Lust of the flesh → sexual immorality, impurity, debauchery, sensuality.

Lust of the eyes → idolatry, sorcery, envy, greed, covetousness.

Pride of life → hatred, selfish ambition, fits of rage, strife, divisions, heresies.

Evil does not only act; it communicates. It has a semantic field of expression—meaning it operates through a network of thoughts, words, attitudes, behaviors, and cultural patterns that convey its influence. Just as language reveals intent, evil expresses itself through recognizable patterns once discernment is developed.

Jesus confirms this in John 8:44, saying that when the devil lies, he speaks his native language. Lies, manipulation, and distortion of truth are expressions of evil's rebellion. Evil seeks not only to act, but to persuade, influence, and mislead hearts and minds away from God's truth.

The mission of evil is destruction. Jesus states this plainly in John 10:10: *"The thief comes only to steal and kill and destroy."* Evil aims to damage what belongs to God, harm His creation, and disrupt His purpose. However, not every challenge is evil. Some trials are permitted for growth, refinement, and obedience.

Finally, Scripture clarifies the true nature of our conflict. Ephesians 6:12 says, *"For we do not wrestle against flesh and blood, but against rulers, authorities, powers of this dark world, and spiritual forces of evil in the heavenly realms."* Evil operates through organized spiritual structures. Recognizing this allows us to stand firm, resist deception, and engage spiritual conflict with clarity about the true enemy.

Chapter 4 — Discovering What Is Good

In the previous chapter, we explored evil—what it is, where it comes from, and how it manifests in the world and in our hearts. It gives us a necessary foundation, but to truly walk in truth, we must also understand what is genuinely good.

True goodness is defined exclusively by God. Everything that is truly good originates from Him, reflects His nature, and aligns with His will. Before we can fully recognize and embrace this standard of good, let us return to the concept of renewing the mind. Again, I am trying to make you practice something you will practice outside of this book.

In this chapter, we will explore the goodness of God, the qualities He values, and how His unchanging nature defines what is truly good. By examining Scripture and understanding the heart of God, we will learn to test, compare, and approve what aligns with His truth, so that our lives may reflect His goodness in every action, thought, and choice.

As we established in Section 2, Chapter 1, renewing the mind is fundamental to many layers of the Christian experience. It is what allows us to measure everything against God's eternal standard.

But how does this actually happen? Romans 12:2 gives us a clear answer. In the wording of this passage, we are told that *"then you will be able to test and approve what God's will is—His good, pleasing, and perfect will."* The Amplified version emphasizes this by saying, *"so that you may prove [for yourselves] what the will of God is, that which is good and acceptable and perfect [in His plan and purpose for you]."*

This reveals specific capacities that must be developed so we can test, compare, and approve for ourselves God's goodness—goodness that is whole, perfect, and unchanging. Let us develop these capacities together.

Testing is the careful examination of something to uncover its true weight, value, and integrity. Scripture often uses the image of refining metals by fire to illustrate the process in which heat remains until impurities are exposed and removed. Proverbs 17:3 says, *"The refining pot is for silver and the furnace for gold, but the LORD tests the hearts."*

In Romans 12:2, the Greek word translated as *"to test"* is *dokimazō (δοκιμάζω)*. It means to test, examine, prove, or scrutinize in order to determine whether something is genuine.

To test is to hold something up before God's light, apply His standard to it, and allow its true essence to be revealed. It asks the question, "Does this carry weight in eternity, or is it hollow?"

Comparing and proving bring clarity and discernment. While testing reveals quality, this step requires us to weigh two or more things against each other and distinguish what is aligned with God's truth from what is counterfeit. First Thessalonians 5:21–22 says, *"Test everything; hold fast what is good. Abstain from every form of evil."* Again, the Greek word *dokimazō* is used, this time emphasizing proving by contrast—discerning, distinguishing, and recognizing true value. It is related to *diakrinō*, meaning "to judge between" or "to make a distinction.

Testing exposes, proving separates, but **Approving** brings the matter home. Approving means more than simply recognizing what is good; it means wholeheartedly embracing it as your personal conviction. You do not live off borrowed truth—you affirm and accept God's will as your own. Philippians 1:10 says, *"So that you may approve the things that are excellent, in order to be sincere and blameless until the day of Christ."* Here, *dokimazō* carries its full depth: not just to test, but to recognize, approve, and embrace as excellent. It also carries the nuance of *sugkatathesis*—agreement, consent, and personal assent.

The key to testing, comparing, and approving requires an outside perspective—certainly not our own flawed, carnal reasoning. That higher perspective is called truth, or the knowledge of God. I define this as **Kingdom-critical thinking**.

The practical application of renewing the mind begins when we intentionally set aside our personal definitions, cultural assumptions, and emotional responses to allow God to define "good" according to His own nature. This foundational shift takes us back to the very first evaluation in Scripture: the dawn of creation. As the light broke the void, the Word records, *"And God saw the light, that it was good; and God divided the light from the darkness"* (Genesis 1:4). This moment is pivotal because it establishes that the standard of goodness does not originate from humanity observing the world; it comes from God Himself evaluating His work. From the beginning, God defined what is good and what is not, independent of any human perception.

To truly renew our thinking, we must embrace the language God used. The Hebrew word translated as good is *ṭôb*—a term that moves us far beyond the shallow idea of something being merely "nice." *Ṭôb* carries a weight of divine judgment, revealing God's original intent for a finished creation. It encompasses all that is beneficial, beautiful, fruitful, and useful; it speaks of a harmony where everything functions exactly as it was designed to function. In the Genesis record, we see that *ṭôb* describes a blessing that is generative. Vegetation, for instance, is not called *ṭôb* simply because it exists, but because it is capable of reproducing. Here, the renewal of the mind becomes concrete: we learn that "*good*" is defined by how well a thing can produce according to its God-given function.

Instead of asking whether a situation feels pleasant or benefits us immediately, we are taught to ask whether it reflects God's design and produces life according to His order. Ultimately, to call something good is to declare that it aligns with divine integrity. When a thing reflects His holiness, truth, love, and justice, it is *ṭôb*.

Conversely, when it distorts or rebels against that intent, it reflects something foreign to His nature—the very definition of evil. But the renewal of the mind is not complete until this definition becomes our primary tool for evaluation. It is not enough to know what *ṭôb* means; we must begin to measure our own conclusions against it.

This is where many believers struggle, for we often label things as *"good"* simply because they bring relief, offer comfort, or align with our personal desires. Yet, renewed thinking demands a different question. It does not ask, "Do I like this?" or "Does this benefit me now?" It asks, "Does this align with God's definition? Does God judge this as good?" As you carry your cross and love the Lord with your mind, a transformation begins to take place within you. Your preferences shift. What once attracted you loses its pull, and what once felt difficult begins to make sense. You start to love what God loves and hate what God hates.

If a thing is truly good, it must lead toward wholeness, not compromise; it must produce life, not just temporary relief. This comparison often requires letting go of conclusions we have held for a long time. Some things we have called "*good*" must be reclassified, and some paths we pursued in the name of "blessing" must be examined again. This is not a loss; it is a correction and a holy alignment. When our definitions are brought into agreement with *ṭôb,* our discernment becomes clear. We are no longer led by emotion or appearance, but by truth, walking in a way that truly reflects the goodness of the Father.

We so often miss the goodness of God because we forget that it was always present. We mistakenly believe that knowledge is born at the moment we discover it, yet discovery is simply the human mind catching up to what God has already established. Even time itself is nothing more than stretched mercy—a corridor in which God allows humanity to gradually unfold what He has already finished. The problem is not that God's goodness is unclear; it is that our perception is too narrow. We have been trained to expect His goodness only in spectacular forms that we label "supernatural," reducing it to rare and dramatic encounters like Moses standing before the burning bush. Because of this limited framework, we overlook the constant presence of God's goodness woven into the very fabric of everyday life.

We must realize that the rising of the sun each morning is supernatural and a vital part of the goodness of God. The unseen systems within the human body that govern reproduction and healing are supernatural and a part of that same goodness. Even medicine is supernatural—not in opposition to God, but as an access point to His wisdom and resurrection power. I could go on for hours about how this allows humanity to interact with the design He placed within creation. This goodness is a testimony to me, and I pray it becomes a testimony to you, as it stands as a witness to His character.

What we call science is merely the human attempt to describe, with limited language, the vast order and wisdom of God's creation. What we call technology is humanity borrowing from the mind of God to produce tools that reflect His creativity. What we call medicine is our participation in His healing power, while government reflects His order, and psychology offers a fragment of discernment applied to the inner life of man.

In reality, all of these are expressions of God's goodness woven into the world. The error arises when we separate them, labeling some as "human goodness" and reserving others as "God's goodness." This separation is rooted in pride; it darkens our perception and distorts our view of God as the Source, falsely elevating humanity as the judge of what belongs to Him. This disorder leads us to divide what God has authored, forgetting that every good and perfect gift is from above.

When perception is distorted, goodness is misidentified. **Clarity regarding God's goodness requires knowing God Himself.** Until His nature becomes our only reference point, we will continue to misread His hand.

How we interpret trials reveals whether our knowing of God's goodness is truly rooted in Him or merely in our own convenience. Proverbs 3:5 urges us to trust in the Lord with all our heart and to lean not on our own understanding.

To trust the Lord in this way is to refuse the old, human framework of thought.

The challenge, then, is to learn how to test every experience—to see our trials, blessings, and events from God's perspective. This is the heart of what James teaches when he tells us to consider it pure joy when we face trials of many kinds. He reveals that the testing of our faith produces perseverance, and when perseverance finishes its work, God calls that *"good"* because it produces a profitable outcome. We become mature and complete, lacking nothing.

A person who knows that goodness belongs to God does not allow emotions or superficial perceptions to define their reality. Instead, they examine every situation for its alignment with God's standard. Even in the midst of hardship, they can declare a season *"good"* because they see it producing something that matches God's design.

Ultimately, most of us respond to trials based on feelings, but ignorance of God's nature is the enemy's greatest advantage. He thrives when we are confused and unable to discern the truth of God's goodness. A lack of discernment makes it easy for the thief to destroy our faith and steal what we do not know we possess.

However, the knowledge of God's nature is protective. It equips us to navigate life with clarity, purpose, and a confidence that cannot be shaken. With this foundation, every description of God's goodness becomes more than a word—it becomes a snapshot of His behavior and His will. Every trial and every victory is then viewed through this lens, allowing us to recognize His hand in all things and grow into the fullness of who He created us to be.

Section III

The Origin of Satan

Chapter 1 — But Who Is Satan? Who Was Lucifer?

Spiritual Warfare is fundamentally about understanding who we are truly dealing with. Many people talk about Spiritual Warfare, but few genuinely discern—or clearly explain—the enemy's structure. We are in a war against Satan, and that war is spiritual in nature.

There is no better place to start a spiritual war than by knowing the integrity of the thing you are battling against. We do this by shining the light of truth onto Satan and his schemes. Casting out demons or speaking in tongues is powerful, remarkable, and effective—especially when done properly. That being said, we cannot start and finish with only that.

Spiritual Warfare is essentially about knowing the origin of evil and its progression. Before you go to war, you plan. You need to know your adversary. This means perceiving evil from God's standpoint, recognizing what is truly good, and renewing your mind so you remain alert against the schemes of the devil.

Furthermore, it is about knowing the one who orchestrates it all, and the system he builds around it. And the system Satan is building is, in fact, falling apart. If we take the time to turn the light on—and keep it on—we would see this for ourselves.

Spiritual Warfare is dangerously incomplete without investigating Satan. Many believers fight in the dark and in the flesh because they have not taken the time to examine the satanic structure. They often mistakenly believe that learning about something equates to glorifying it. This is incorrect. Knowing the true nature of something glorifies God, not the thing itself—whether it is good or evil.

Let's talk about Satan and his beginning, because we need to be clear on this: Lucifer and Satan are not the same. God made Lucifer —perfect, radiant, anointed, and honored. Through rebellion, Lucifer became Satan. This change in descriptor shows how someone created in glory becomes corrupted. It ends one life and begins another—one who now stands against God in defeat.

Before we go deeper into Satan's agenda or structure, I want to begin with his origin. Because when we unpack where evil began, we gain clarity on how it operates—and how it takes root within us. From God's point of view, evil is anything that stands in opposition to Him.

Evil has an origin—it began with pride and rebellion (Isaiah 14:12–15).
Evil has a substance—iniquity gives it form and expression (Galatians 5:18, 22; James 1:15).
Evil has a method—it speaks, deceives, and lies (John 8:44).
Evil has an agenda—to steal, kill, and destroy (John 10:10).
Evil has a structure—rulers, authorities, and powers of darkness (Ephesians 6:12).

But before evil became a system, it began as a seed—planted in a heart that was once glorious. That heart belonged to Lucifer. So who was Lucifer?

The first mention of Lucifer appears in Isaiah 14:12:

"How art thou fallen from heaven, O Lucifer, son of the morning! How art thou cut down to the ground, which didst weaken the nations!"

Other translations refer to him as the "morning star" or the "shining one," emphasizing the brilliance and honor he once carried. Ezekiel gives us further insight in Ezekiel 28:14:

"You were the anointed guardian cherub. I placed you; you were on the holy mountain of God; in the midst of the stones of fire you walked."

This gives us a clearer picture of who Lucifer was created by God to be. He was an **anointed guardian cherub**. That phrase alone describes his function, his position, and his authority under God's design.

Let's begin with the word **anointed**. The first mention of anointing in Scripture appears in Genesis 31:13, where it says, *"I am the God of Bethel, where thou anointest the pillar..."* In that moment, Jacob poured oil on a stone to set it apart as sacred. It was a physical act of consecration.

To anoint means to set something apart for divine purpose—to consecrate it for God's use. The Hebrew word for anoint is *māshach*, meaning *to smear, to rub with oil, to consecrate*. From this root comes *Mashiach*, meaning *"The Anointed One"*—the Messiah. In Greek, the word is *chriō*, from which we get *Christos*, or *Christ*, meaning *"The Anointed One."*

41

So when Ezekiel tells us that Lucifer was *anointed*, it means he was set apart by God Himself. He was prepared and empowered for a sacred, holy assignment. Lucifer was not created to oppose God. He was created to serve within God's order. But anointing does not remove free will. You can be set apart and still choose rebellion.

The second word used to describe Lucifer is **guardian**. The first time we see this concept in Scripture is in Genesis 2:15: "And the Lord God took the man, and put him into the garden of Eden to dress it and to keep it." The word keep in Hebrew is **shāmar**. It means to guard, to preserve, to protect. It carries the sense of covering something precious—of hedging it in and keeping it safe.

Lucifer was an anointed guardian—one entrusted to protect what was holy, to preserve divine order, and to shield the presence of God. His role was to protect glory, not to seek it for himself. You are never meant to take advantage of what you are called to guard. The moment you do, you stop protecting it. That is where corruption begins.

The final word used to describe Lucifer's title is *cherub*. The first time the word *cherub* appears in Scripture is in Genesis 3:24. The verse says, *"So He drove out the man; and He placed at the east of the garden of Eden cherubim, and a flaming sword..."* Cherubim are heavenly beings assigned to guard the presence of God. They are protectors of holiness, defenders of divine space, and living symbols of God's authority and purity.

The Hebrew word **kerūb** is believed to come from the Akkadian **karābu**, meaning *to bless* or *to praise*. These beings are not ordinary angels. They belong to the highest order surrounding God's throne.

Lucifer was one of them—a **covering cherub**. He stood close to the throne, among the fiery stones, surrounded by God's glory. He had access to wisdom, knowledge, and God's authority. He understood God's order and nature. Lucifer moved within the rhythm of divine worship itself.

Yet despite all of this—perfect beauty, divine access, and holy anointing—pride took root. Ezekiel 28:16–18 tells us:

"By the abundance of your trading, you became filled with violence within, and you sinned. Therefore, I cast you as a profane thing out of the mountain of God... Your heart was lifted up because of your beauty; you corrupted your wisdom for the sake of your splendor."

Lucifer's heart shifted. He exalted himself because of his own beauty—not sacred beauty, but vain beauty. How long must one gaze inward before feeling worthy of exaltation above the Creator? In that moment, his essence changed. He was made to cover the throne, yet he sought to occupy it. That marked the end of Lucifer and the beginning of Satan.

When corruption entered him, his nature was negated, and his actions followed. He could no longer carry a name that reflected light. He became its opposite. Lucifer ended the moment pride was conceived within him. It is like pure water mixed with lemon juice —once combined, it can no longer be called water. The substance has changed. Lucifer was altered by iniquity, and that altered nature gave birth to Satan.

This is one of the enemy's greatest deceptions: he still pretends to hold his former position. Across cultures, he presents himself as an angel of light. But the truth is simple—Lucifer died the day he lifted his heart in pride. *"Your heart was lifted up because of your beauty"* (Ezekiel 28:17). That self-exaltation became the root of Satan's existence.

Pride produces rebellion. Lucifer became Satan. His nature shifted—from guardian to adversary, from light-bearer to destroyer.

Chapter 2—Understanding The Person of Satan

Now that we have seen how Lucifer ceased to exist, we are left with Satan. He remains active, deceptive, and strategic—but he is nowhere near as great or as powerful as he pretends to be.

Make no mistake: Satan constantly pushes his own narrative. He is the prince of pride, the fountain of boasting and arrogance. He admired his own beauty and used his words to exalt himself. From the moment of his fall, he began crafting his own story, his own definitions, and his own ideas.

If you study the Satanic Bible or examine the teachings of those who follow him, you will notice a consistent message. It is the same rebellion and the same ancient lies, simply dressed in attractive language. People see the sparkle and mistake it for light, but it is only a shadow pretending to shine.

Throughout history, occult and esoteric systems have presented Satan as the "bringer of knowledge," the one who frees humanity from God's order, or even as a spiritual guide. No matter the vocabulary, the agenda never changes: invert God's structure, glorify self, and elevate rebellion above submission.

Satan portrays himself as a liberator. He claims to free humanity from what he calls God's "chains." He presents himself as the source of wisdom and understanding—a ruler who rejects authority and calls it freedom. He gives people what they desire and labels it as good. He casts himself as both victim and victor—oppressed and exalted. He displays beauty, success, power, and freedom. He rules a kingdom served by demons. Some even imagine hell as a party, believing they are greater than God and worthier than Jesus.

But all of this is seductive deception. In order to mislead, Satan must first distort the truth. This is why knowing God—His character, His order, and His ways—is essential. Deception can only succeed where truth is unknown, unstudied, or ignored.

The very first strategy recorded in Scripture, in the Garden of Eden, reveals his method clearly: **twist the truth, appeal to desire, encourage self-exaltation over obedience** (Genesis 3:5), and then label the rebellion as good.

Every lie Satan promotes aims at one goal: to be seen as Christ without ever submitting to God. This pattern repeats itself throughout false religions, philosophies, and modern spiritual movements that separate holiness from obedience. Some systems separate Christ's consciousness from His person, presenting a mystical and abstract idea of redemption with no cross and no submission. Gnosticism, ancient mysticism, and today's spiritual ideologies all follow the same blueprint: imitate redemption while rejecting obedience, imitate light while removing holiness, and copy God's order while denying His nature. If you do not know the truth that belongs to God, you will not recognize the subtle differences.

To further expose these deceptive spiritualities, we must examine the carefully crafted language they use to mislead. These systems redefine spiritual concepts in ways completely disconnected from Scripture. They instruct people to "look within" for truth, unaware that making the self the source of revelation is the same lie that initiated Satan's own rebellion.

Self-exaltation becomes the doorway he walks through, because the moment truth is separated from God, it becomes deception by default.

When you look to the self as the ultimate source of truth, you are no longer looking to God. Instead, you are aligning with the very lie Satan used from the beginning. People search for truth in the wrong direction and are then surprised when they arrive in Hell. They believe they are discovering truth for themselves, when in reality they have been subtly led to that conclusion through a specific teaching framework crafted by the enemy.

This is similar to those who conclude that Christianity is false because they have studied only secular interpretations of religious history. They did not *discover* that Christianity was false; they were guided to that conclusion through a syllabus designed to shape their thinking. And when you ask them whether they have read the entire Bible, the answer is usually no.

In literature, you cannot form a legitimate conclusion about a manuscript you have never studied or cross-examined with truthful tools. That, too, is deception—and Satan is a master of it.

Many who identify as *"spiritual"* believe they are called to become like God Himself. This is false. We are called to be like Jesus Christ, not God the Father. The difference may appear small in wording, but it is massive in truth. Misunderstanding this distinction can lead a person directly into destruction. Lucifer was close to God, yet Satan became the father of lies.

Satan's influence is subtle, pervasive, and relational—like the wind. He does not operate alone. He works through human desires, weaknesses, and ignorance of truth. Every deception succeeds only when it is accepted—whether through agreement, neglect, or pride.

Comprehending this is critical because it reveals that spiritual warfare is not primarily a battle against visible forces, but a resistance against the strategies of a deceiver who knows how to exploit every opportunity to bend creation away from God.

The meaning of the word *Satan* is more a revelation of failure than an actual name. In Hebrew, *śāṭān (שָׂטָן)* means *adversary, accuser, or opponent*. It describes a function, not a position of honor. When Lucifer fell, he lost his name. He lost identity, glory, and honor—everything that once tied him to divine purpose. What was once Lucifer, the light-bearer, became Satan, the adversary.

Here we see the first contradiction of who Satan is. He wanted to rise above God, yet his very designation means *the one who stands against*. He wanted to ascend, but his identification testifies that he was cast down. He wanted to be worshiped, but his denomination exposed how unworthy he is of worship. He wanted to be like God, yet his very epithet declares the opposite.

In Greek, **Satanas** carries the same meaning: *the accuser*, the one who opposes the divine will. Every time Scripture uses the word *Satan*, it is not granting him a title of greatness. It reminds us of rebellion, failure, and defeat. The label itself marks one who exchanged the glory of heaven for shame and corruption.

In the spiritual realm, names are never empty. They carry identity and authority. When God names something, He defines its nature. When Adam named the animals, he assigned identity. When God renamed Abram to Abraham, or Jacob to Israel, the new name carried promise and purpose.

In the same way, when Lucifer fell, heaven stripped him of his former name according to his corruption. He forfeited his identity and was left with a title that exposed his rebellion.

Satan does not want to be known by what he became; he wants to be called by what he pretends to be. He rejects being seen as the adversary and prefers titles like enlightened one, liberator, or god of this age. He crafts images and names that disguise his true nature—*Morning Star, Bringer of Light, Spirit of Knowledge, Voice of Freedom*. These are counterfeits designed to make you forget what his appellation actually means.

When you repeat Satan's narrative by calling him what he wants to be called, you empower his lie. You give him agreement, and agreement is spiritual permission. He feeds on recognition, validation, and subtle forms of worship. This is why his greatest goal is not always possession, but persuasion. He wants to persuade you to see him as harmless, wise, or even helpful.

That is why, in this book, we are learning who Satan truly is and rejecting the way he boasts about himself. His descriptor reveals his fall, while his lies are designed to hide it. Believing his boasting is participating in his rebellion. Seeing him through God's eyes strips him of influence.

Revelation 12:10 identifies him clearly as *"the accuser of our brethren, who accused them before God day and night."* That is his true nature. He is not a liberator, not light, not a misunderstood victim. He is the embodiment of contradiction.

Every time you agree with his self-portrait, you return to him what he lost in heaven: recognition. But when you call him what God calls him—adversary, accuser, deceiver—you reclaim authority. You put him where he belongs: under judgment, beneath authority, and outside of glory.

Understanding the meaning of his identification is not merely theological information; it is spiritual warfare. You cannot defeat what you continue to admire. You cannot cast down what you secretly agree with. To learn his true epithet is to expose his mask, reject his narrative, and reclaim your discernment.

Satan calls himself *"free,"* offering the illusion that freedom means doing whatever you please—indulging every desire, breaking every boundary, and living without restraint. But true freedom is the power to live free from bondage and sin. It is found in obedience to truth, for *"the truth shall set you free"* (John 8:32). God calls him fallen, because the "freedom" Satan presents is rebellion—a fallen perspective that ultimately leads to captivity.

Satan does not call himself light in Scripture, but the Bible reveals something even more dangerous: he imitates light. Paul warns us in 2 Corinthians 11:14 that *"Satan himself masquerades as an angel of light."* This means he disguises himself in forms that resemble enlightenment, wisdom, healing, or self-discovery—but it is counterfeit illumination, designed to pull the soul away from God.

As mentioned before, one of the primary ways Satan imitates light is through philosophies that teach, "Look within," "Find your own light," or "You are your own source of truth." This form of self-centered spirituality makes the self the ultimate authority. But the moment the self becomes the source, the door opens for Satan to influence, deceive, and occupy that inner space.

The fallen nature becomes the lens, and Satan manipulates it easily because it mirrors his own rebellion. When the enemy encourages you to look inward for enlightenment apart from God, he is not revealing light—he is offering a polished version of darkness. It feels empowering, but it leads to confusion, fragmentation, and spiritual blindness.

True light does not come from within us. True light is Christ Himself. In the Kingdom, love, truth, and light are spiritual synonyms, and all three originate in Him. We recognize authentic light by its fruit: it casts out darkness, exposes lies, heals wounds, restores moral order, and brings freedom.

Darkness cannot remove darkness. The self cannot illuminate the self. Only Jesus can fill the inner space with real light. The light of Christ comes from outside of us—holy, uncreated, uncontaminated —and God invites us to receive it into the empty spaces of our soul.

When His light enters, every counterfeit light is exposed, and every shadow must flee. This is how we remain protected from the deception of one who pretends to shine, yet carries only darkness within himself.

God calls him darkness because the substance he offers blinds. Darkness is the substance of demonic oppression and torment, pulling the soul into deep ignorance. A person can be full of information and still be spiritually blind. When the result of that information leads to death, it reveals its origin in darkness.

God never calls Satan a liberator. God never calls him a giver of truth. God never portrays him as misunderstood—so why would we? Why would we accept a version of him that God Himself rejects?

Recognizing Satan as Scripture reveals him also enables us to distinguish the true Jesus from counterfeits. Satan imitates Christ's work, voice, and appearance of light, but his nature is the opposite. He corrupts instead of heals, manipulates instead of restores, and seeks dominion without submission. Learning how God describes Satan teaches us to identify these imitations and refuse them before they take root.

Every behavior God hates is rooted in Satan's nature. When we know him through God's lens, we begin to recognize those same traits in ourselves and in the world—and that recognition gives us the power to reject them. Every time we identify those patterns, we prevent Satan from taking root. Every time we refuse the titles he desires, we deny him authority.

When we perceive Satan as God describes him, we gain the ability to detect corruption, deception, and rebellion wherever they appear. We discern false teachings quickly. This is how we enforce the victory Christ has already secured.

Learning how God describes Satan sharpens our discernment in leadership, authority, and influence. Individuals who move in pride, manipulation, or accusation often reflect the spirit of the adversary. Recognizing this empowers us to correct, remove, or intercede over these influences, protecting ourselves and others from corruption.

It also exposes the subtle nature of deception. At the same time, it magnifies God's holiness, the beauty of obedience, and the strength found in submission. Knowing the enemy as God defines him teaches us both what to resist and how to align ourselves with the Kingdom of Light, so we can walk in authority over darkness. This knowledge becomes spiritual armor—discernment becomes the lens through which both the enemy and the Kingdom of God are revealed with clarity.

Satan has power, but he does not have authority. We must be absolutely clear about this, because this distinction shapes everything. His power exists, but it is restricted and can only manifest in limited and specific ways. His power is not divine; it is corruptive. It is not creative; it contaminates. It is not sovereign; it is strategically selfish. And it is not equal to God in any measure.

Within the Body of Christ, this truth is often neglected— sometimes out of fear, sometimes out of ignorance, and sometimes simply because it has not been taught. We boldly declare that "Satan is defeated," and that declaration is true. But many stop there and never learn that Christ's victory must be applied in order to become effective in their individual lives.

The victory of the cross was completed on earth in a specific moment of time, yet it was established in eternity before the foundation of the world. Jesus secured that victory in both the spiritual and natural realms for all time. However, its effectiveness in our daily lives is activated through spiritual maturity and submission to God.

Some may say, "If Satan is defeated, then there is nothing left for me to do." But that is incorrect. Satan was defeated outside of time, yet the application of Christ's victory unfolds within time, through your growth in spiritual authority. In the natural realm, things are still moving, changing, and responding to your choices.

Christ's victory is not automatic in experience; it must be applied and activated through submission to salvation, through coherent perception of the truth that belongs to God, and through obedience to His order. Spiritual maturity is demonstrated when you see the Kingdom, the Word, and the workings of the universe through God's perspective—including a clear and balanced comprehension of Satan's limited power.

Think of it this way: a criminal may be imprisoned, yet still run operations from behind prison walls because those outside remain ignorant of the law. This is how Satan operates. He is judged and bound, yet his influence spreads—not through divine authority, but through human ignorance. Ignorance becomes a weapon he uses against people, a chain that can bind entire generations (Ephesians 4:18).

Satan continues to operate because he feeds on what we neglect to learn—God's structure, God's order, and God's systems. Structure is how God organizes creation and life, the divine framework that holds everything together. God's order is the proper alignment, sequence, and priority of all things according to His will—the harmony that exists when everything is in its rightful place. God's systems are the spiritual laws and divine patterns through which He governs the universe, the processes that consistently reveal His wisdom and His ways. And the integrity of a thing is the discovery of why a thing or a being exists through the lens of God—its identity, purpose, and divine order as He designed it.

When we ignore these truths, we create a deficiency in our cognitive conceptual mental processing (the ability to receive, organize, interpret, and understand information). Satan studies those deficiencies. He observes where we refuse to learn, where we remain unsubmitted, and where we remain unaware. Then he weaponizes that neglect against us.

By twisting the truths we ignore, Satan manipulates us into surrendering authority that never belonged to him. Through deception, he convinces us to unknowingly sign away our own power. He is like a dry, empty shelf attempting to rebuild a kingdom from leftover fragments of what he once knew—using memories of former glory to construct counterfeit visions inside the human mind.

Satan's power is borrowed power. Stop lending him your authority. Stop lending him your dominion. He is like a dead insect that lost its wings but still remembers how to fly. He can no longer soar, yet he knows how to persuade others to surrender their wings. He whispers, *"I can make you fly."* When you believe him, you unknowingly sign away your authority—your wings—granting him permission to operate in your life, your family, and your generational line.

He elevates people briefly to create a false sense of accomplishment, only to crash them back down so they remain dependent on him. That is the essence of deception. Satan's power does not come from creation, strength, or sovereignty. It comes from strategy and manipulation. He is not foolish. He is a fallen, supernatural being—structured, observant, and organized. He is not inherently more powerful than you, but when we refuse to learn, grow, understand, and live according to God's truth, we give him influence in our lives.

Before his rebellion, Satan—then known as Lucifer—stood in the presence of God. He was radiant, full of wisdom, adorned with precious stones, and entrusted with divine music and spiritual order (Ezekiel 28:13). When he fell, he was cut off from the Source of life, but he did not lose his knowledge of divine order. Ezekiel 28:17 says.

"Your heart was lifted up because of your beauty; you corrupted your wisdom for the sake of your splendor; I cast you to the ground..."

This means he did not lose his wisdom; he corrupted it. He twisted what remained and weaponized it to build a system of darkness. He knows how divine authority functions. He knows how obedience activates power. He imitates God's structure, perverting it to construct a counterfeit kingdom over human lives. His power is sustained by what he steals: human dominion, ignorance, and consent.

Since Adam's fall, humanity has been his primary source of strength. He cannot create—he can only corrupt. He cannot bless—he can only counterfeit. He cannot rule—he can only manipulate those who were given authority. His kingdom may appear clever and strategic, but it is fragile, like a house of cards.

This is why God calls His people to wisdom and discernment. Proverbs 4:7 declares, *"Wisdom is the principal thing; therefore get wisdom. And in all your getting, get understanding."* You cannot overthrow a system you do not recognize. You cannot conquer what you refuse to confront. And you cannot walk in freedom if you do not recognize what enslaves you.

Knowing Satan in the light of Jesus reveals the true nature of spiritual warfare. This knowledge brings freedom and establishes Christ's victory in your life. Spiritual warfare is not fear-driven combat; it is the daily enforcement of Satan's defeat in every area of your existence by seeing him as God reveals him—through truth, not fear.

The purpose of this book is not to glorify the enemy, but to expose his system, overturn ignorance, and dismantle deception. We are here to strip him of every illusion of power.

Once you realize that Satan's power depends entirely on human cooperation, you begin to see how much authority God truly gave you. Satan cannot move without participation. He must be invited, believed, or obeyed to operate. When you grasp this, fear loses its grip. You stop reacting and begin ruling. You stop repeating his lies and start enforcing the truth.

Satan's power is real, but it is fading. It feeds on darkness produced by ignorance, pride, and rebellion. But the moment the light of enlightenment enters, it collapses. John 1:5 declares, *"The light shines in the darkness, and the darkness did not comprehend it."* Every believer who learns the truth becomes a point of collapse for the kingdom of darkness.

The power of Satan is not to be denied, but it is not to be feared. It is to be understood, dissected, discerned, and overcome daily. James 4:7 lays out this principle plainly:

"Therefore, submit to God. Resist the devil, and he will flee from you."

Chapter 3 — Understanding His Access – The Choir of Angels

Before man was created, God had already established a divine order in heaven. Every angelic being was created with an assignment, a position, and a sound that reflected the glory of God.

In this chapter, we study the divine order Satan attempted to counterfeit. Scripture shows us that he once had high access within God's heavenly structure. Ezekiel 28:14–15 reveals that Lucifer walked on the holy mountain of God and moved in the midst of the fiery stones. This describes proximity, not omnipotence.

Isaiah 14:12–14 shows that his rebellion came from the desire to rise higher, which means he was already positioned close to glory. Job 1:6–7 further confirms that even after the fall, Satan could still present himself before the Lord. Access existed, but authority did not.

Deconstructing Satan's access helps us recognize the system he now imitates. Without this, we cannot discern the imitation he built from the kingdom he tried to corrupt.

The nine choirs of angels reveal both divine hierarchy and divine system. Angels were not created equal. Each rank carries a different function and a different proximity to the throne of God. The closer the proximity, the purer the exposure to light, wisdom, and knowledge. Angelic beings were created outside of time; they did not grow into their roles—they were formed with them.

So Satan's knowledge did not come from rebellion. Darkness did not grant him new power. His knowledge came from proximity to God. He did not gain insight by falling; he corrupted what he already possessed. Darkness is not an equal source to light, even though Satan has convinced many that it is. What he presents as a new revelation is an ancient truth twisted into deception. This distinction matters. Twisting and creating are not the same. Satan cannot create; he can only corrupt.

His system is built on a misused structure. That is why knowledge of God's order dismantles the web of lies that sustains disorder.

The choirs of angels also reveal something about us. They expose the position God designed for humanity and the same position Satan attempted to steal, kill, and destroy. Which was restored through the blood of Jesus on the altar of salvation. When God's order is clear, Satan's counterfeit becomes obvious and ineffective. Spiritual warfare is not fascination with darkness; it is a deep understanding of divine order. When the structure of God is known, deception loses its footing.

As I write this chapter, I feel the weight of God's glory and the purpose behind every tear, every trial, and every season I have endured. What the enemy meant for harm is becoming a revelation. I pause to give Jesus all the honor, knowing that through these truths, darkness will be defeated in the lives of those who read and hear them.

Studying the Nine Choirs of Angels—their precise hierarchy, function, and structure—completely renewed my mind. I realized that much of what we've been taught about the cosmos has come through a deceptive lens: Satan's counterfeit version of reality. To successfully deceive, one must first know the truth. His lies are packaged in stories, fables, songs, and movies that shape a false reality.

If faith comes by hearing the truth, then we must also recognize that corruption enters through what we hear. This distorted design minimizes God, reducing our perception of His vastness into a powerless version of what we call "religion" or "Christianity." It is no wonder so many people are confused and seek answers elsewhere.

My goal for this book is simple: to let truth shatter long-held lies, to establish the victory of Jesus in your life, and to give God all the glory.

To properly discern truth from falsehood, we must examine the actual, divinely ordained structure of the spiritual realm. The cosmos is not a chaotic accident, but a precise reflection of God's perfect order. When we analyze the authentic blueprint of Heaven's chain of command, we reclaim a vital piece of God's revealed reality. This structure is best understood through what theologians call the **Three Spheres of the Angelic Hierarchy**.

A sphere is not merely a place, but a dimension of proximity and function within God's creation. Heaven is structured. Everything moves in alignment with God's will. Each sphere reflects a facet of God's nature, and each choir within it carries a role, a function, and a level of access to His glory.

The classification of the nine choirs into three spheres comes from early theological study, primarily the work of Pseudo-Dionysius the Areopagite.

The first sphere is closest to God. These are the counselors, worshipers, and guardians of divine wisdom. The second sphere consists of the managers of creation—the governors of heaven and the maintainers of cosmic order. The third sphere hosts the messengers to humanity. These angels deliver God's word, guard people, and execute His plans on the earth.

Every choir mirrors God's holiness, justice, and order. Their placement reveals God's intentional design, including what they are permitted to behold and what authority they are able to carry.

Let us begin with the first sphere of angels—the ones closest to God. This is the sphere known as the **Counselors**. These beings stand nearest to the throne, bearing the weight of divine proximity and reflecting God's nature in purity, wisdom, and justice. Their presence reveals the structure of heaven itself.

The first among them are the **Seraphim**, described as the burning ones. The Hebrew root *śāraph* means *"to burn"* or *"to consume with fire."* This burning is not destruction; it is purity, intensity, and an all-consuming love for God. These beings are entirely overtaken by worship, holiness, and divine fire.

In Isaiah's vision, one of them touches his lips with a burning coal, cleansing him for prophetic ministry. They cry without ceasing, "Holy, holy, holy is the Lord of hosts; the whole earth is full of His glory." Each moment they behold God, they encounter another dimension of His beauty, and their worship rises again. Because they stand closest to His throne, their very nature reflects the raw, unfiltered radiance of His presence.

Next in this sphere are the **Cherubim**, beings associated with the fullness of knowledge and the guardianship of God's mysteries. In Christian theology, the Cherubim represent *scientiae plenitudo*—the fullness of knowledge. Their nearness to God grants them access to His secrets, His sacred spaces, and His divine will.

Scripture describes one of them in Ezekiel, saying, *"You were the anointed cherub who covers... You walked back and forth in the midst of fiery stones."* They also guarded Eden after the fall, holding flaming swords at its entrance. Their role is neither sentimental nor decorative; they have always been entrusted with protecting what is holy and overseeing the revelation of God's will.

Completing the first sphere are the **Thrones**, the embodiment of God's justice and authority. They are envisioned as the very seats upon which His presence and judgment rest. The Thrones represent divine stability and impartial justice—unshakable foundations within heaven's government. They carry out God's decrees across the cosmos, upholding order and maintaining the harmony of creation.

Colossians tells us that all things—whether thrones, dominions, principalities, or powers—were created through Christ and for Christ, making their existence a testimony of God's cosmic rule.

After the first sphere, we step into the next layer of heaven's order. The second sphere contains the angels who manage creation and maintain cosmic order. They rarely reveal themselves directly to humanity, yet their work governs everything from the movement of the cosmos to the alignment of nations.

We begin with the **Dominions**, regulators of order and guardians of divine structure. Their name reflects their role. They ensure that every angel beneath them fulfills its assignment. They receive commands from the Seraphim, Cherubim, and Thrones, and transmit those instructions to the lower ranks without distortion. They maintain cosmic balance, governing spiritual hierarchies with precision. Scripture affirms their place as being far above all principality, power, might, and dominion.

Alongside them are the **Virtues**, the bearers of miracles and grace. Their name, derived from *virtutes*, means "strengths" or "powers." They carry God's strength into creation, influencing natural laws, inspiring courage, and releasing miracles that testify to God's sovereignty. They are channels of divine energy and grace, strengthening humanity to fulfill God's will.

Completing this sphere are the **Powers**, the warriors of the heavenly realm. They stand on the front lines of cosmic conflict, restraining demonic influence, maintaining divine order, and guarding the spiritual pathways that connect creation to the throne. They are not agents of chaos, but enforcers of heaven's justice, standing against corruption and preserving the boundaries God has established.

From here, the order of heaven descends into the sphere most intimately involved with humanity: the **third sphere**. These angels engage directly with the earth, guiding, guarding, and delivering messages from God.

At the highest level of this sphere are the **Principalities**, guardians of nations, territories, and spiritual climates. Their name comes from the Greek *archai*, meaning "rulers" or "first ones." Their role is vast. They oversee nations, cities, cultures, and even areas of scientific advancement, influencing leaders and protecting destinies.

Daniel 10:13 reveals this reality clearly: *"But the prince of the kingdom of Persia withstood me... and Michael, one of the chief princes, came to help me."* This passage exposes the existence of national angels—some loyal to God, others fallen—actively influencing the destinies of nations. The spiritual battles that shape history unfold within this realm.

Next are the **Archangels**, God's chief messengers and leaders in warfare. Their title, *archangelos*, means "chief messenger." They carry messages of the highest importance and lead strategic battles. Gabriel delivers the announcements of Christ's birth (Luke 1). Michael rises in warfare against Satan (Revelation 12:7–9). Jude 1:9 captures Michael's authority when he rebukes the devil over the body of Moses. These are commanders within God's armies.

Finally, we arrive at the order most familiar to us: the **Angels**, the messengers and guardians of humanity. Their name—*angelos* in Greek, *mal'akh* in Hebrew—simply means *"messenger."* They speak to humans, protect them, intervene on their behalf, and execute God's instructions with precision.

Scripture affirms the reality of guardian angels, revealing that each child has an angel who beholds the face of God. Angels watch over individuals, families, churches, and destinies. They are the most direct sign of God's personal involvement in our lives.

So, where was Lucifer among all this? He was a **Cherub**, one among those associated with fullness of knowledge and guardianship of divine mysteries. He was not the only Cherub; he was one among many. And he was not the "angel of music," as is often preached. His assignment was not to create worship, but to guard the glory—so that all expression of worship, sound, and spiritual movement returned to God alone.

He perverted worship by redirecting it toward himself. He was not the leader of the choir; he was part of the system, not its source.

This obsession with making Satan "God's brother" or an equal has caused tremendous confusion in the Church, but Scripture never supports that idea.

This hierarchy also clarifies **humanity's position**. Though angels were created before us, God crowned humanity with a unique purpose and authority: stewardship over creation. Mankind was given dominion—a governance that surpasses that of angels—because angels were created to sustain the world God designed for us. This is why Ephesians 2:6 is so powerful: *we are seated with Christ in heavenly places.*

Lucifer could not fathom that a being made from dust would eventually be exalted above his own station through Christ. Pride poisoned his heart, and he declared, *"I will ascend. I will exalt. I will sit. I will be like the Most High."* But the throne he lusted after can only be reached through humility and obedience—the very qualities he rejected.

His hatred for humanity is rooted in cosmic envy. Humanity carries what he lost: access, relationship, and authority through obedience. His murderous intent, as Jesus explains in John 8:44, began with the desire to destroy the destiny of mankind.

The truth about Satan's access and knowledge is simple: he can only operate according to who he **used to be—Lucifer**. His understanding is limited to the divine structure he once witnessed. He is not all-knowing, not omnipresent, and not omnipotent. His intelligence is historical, not creative. Hell is not a laboratory of new inventions; it is a graveyard of corrupted memories.

Demons operate through distorted fragments of God's order— fragments corrupted because they stopped looking at God and began looking at themselves.

But Christ overturned every throne, every power, and every dominion. Ephesians 1:20–22 declares that Christ is seated far above all principalities and powers—and through Him, so are we. Darkness is limited. Its power is confined and ultimately defeated.

This means you do not fight **for** victory; you fight **from** victory. The angelic hierarchy—both holy and fallen—functions under divine law. Satan's counterfeit system gains power only when we operate in ignorance, fear, or rebellion, granting him authority he was never meant to have.

This chapter is your invitation to reclaim your seat in Christ. When you know your authority, you enforce Christ's victory over every principality and power that once sought to keep humanity in darkness. Step into your dominion. Live out your purpose. Let the truth you have uncovered shatter every lie that once held you captive.

The devil does his worst—but Jesus always wins.

Section IV

The Ministry of Satan

Chapter 1 — Introduction To The Ministry of Satan

When you read the title of this chapter, you may have wondered why I associated the word "ministry" with "Satan." My core thesis is that all demonic activity is deliberate, structured, and exists to serve a distinct, organized goal. As with any organized ministry, the enemy has a method, a direction, and a purpose. We covered the origin previously. Now we will address the direction and objective of this coordinated effort.

This focus led me to use the word 'ministry.' Ministry comes from Latin *ministerium*, meaning '*service*' or '*office.*' I personally define it as when your desire and gift serve Jesus' mission. However, ministry is the action, not the substance. "Ministry" is the application or execution of service, not the inherent quality of the person or the gift itself. We can view this relationship in three parts:

Element	The Substance (The "What")	The Action (The "How")
The Calling	The gift or desire (the potential).	Ministry (the application of that potential)
The Concept	Service (the core value).	Ministry (the act of serving).
The Function	Authority or Power (the endowment).	Ministry (the execution of that authority).

Ultimately, ministry is the tangible expression of service. It is the outward action performed in the real world, using the internal substance of one's gifts, desires, and calling to fulfill a mission. Ministry is not the gift itself; it is what the gift does. It is not the desire itself; it is how that desire moves. It is the execution of a purpose that already exists inside of you.

This is why the Bible speaks of *"the synagogue of Satan"* (Revelation 2:9; 3:9). A synagogue is a gathering with a purpose, an organized place of activity, a structured environment of influence. So when Scripture uses that language, it is not exaggeration; it is revealing that Satan has a coordinated system of service, a counterfeit ministry with actions, duties, and strategies that advance his agenda.

That is precisely why I am using the word ministry in this chapter. First, to open your eyes to the reality that some of you may believe you are doing ministry for God, when in truth you may be serving yourself, and when the self becomes the center, Satan becomes the beneficiary. Self-ministry is the most subtle doorway into deception because it looks good, feels good, and sounds holy, yet it rejects obedience and sacrifice.

Second, I am using this word because my goal is to expose Satan comprehensively. The purpose of this book is to reveal how he works so you can recognize his strategies, identify his patterns, and refuse his influence with clarity.

Like every ministry, the ministry of Satan has a clear operating system. His aim is to operate a full, parallel kingdom built in the counterfeit of God's perfect order. At the core lies his obsession with dominion and generational alliance. Simply put, Satan wants what man has. He seeks to establish and maintain a presence on earth, hijacking our God-given dominion.

He does this in two key ways.

The first is through usurping authority. When Adam and Eve sinned, they legally handed over the governing authority of the earth to Satan. What God had entrusted to humanity was suddenly transferred into the hands of the adversary, allowing him to influence the world as the "kingdom of darkness." He did not gain this dominion by power; he gained it through human agreement. Sin became the doorway through which Satan could operate, because spiritual authority always follows alignment. Wherever disobedience is present, the enemy takes the seat that was emptied.

The second way he strengthens his influence is by constructing a parallel world, a counterfeit system built through generational alliances, covenants, and agreements. Some are made knowingly in rebellion; others are formed unknowingly through ignorance, trauma, or inherited patterns. But each agreement extends his reach. These alliances allow Satan to weave a shadow version of God's order, a world that mirrors his own rebellion and spreads through human participation across time. This parallel kingdom is not sustained by his power but by the consent of those who align with him, knowingly or unknowingly. It is a kingdom built through cooperation, not creation.

The enemy's mandate is to steal, kill, and destroy. Jesus Himself defined the enemy's threefold mission in John 10:10: *"The thief comes only to steal and kill and destroy."* This is not a general description; it is the operational strategy he uses to extend his will across both spiritual and physical territories. His tools to accomplish this mandate are witchcraft, generational curses, deception, and lies. These methods are used to form spiritual contracts and demonic transactions that become legally binding within spiritual courtrooms. Generational curses and spiritual contracts—often entered into unknowingly through sin or occult practices—provide him with legal entry points, or footholds, into lives and families.

The enemy employs principalities, powers, and demons to carry out his work. These spiritual agents are assigned to execute his will on the earth, operating within a perverse hierarchy of darkness. Ephesians 6:12 defines them as organized ranks against which we wrestle. They are focused and relentless, driven by a single mission: to turn humanity in opposition to the will of God. Satan targets those who are valued by God, using humanity as a means to ultimately wound Him.

The vision of Satan's ministry to be like God (Isaiah 14:14). Every structure, obsession, mandate, tool, and employee mentioned above advances this singular, perverse aim. Satan is working to build a kingdom—**a Parallel World**—where he is like God, worshipped. To dismantle this highly organized "ministry" of darkness, we must first understand it. You cannot defeat what you do not expose, and you cannot expose what you do not understand. In the chapters ahead, we will break down how these systems function and, most importantly, how you can operate in the superior authority of Christ to shut them down.

Chapter 2 — The Evolution of Satan Ministry

Around ten years ago, I began having vivid dreams in which God revealed to me maps of hell. These visions were not chaotic or confusing. They were detailed blueprints showing different layers and dimensions of that realm. I immediately understood its structure, though I initially lacked the words to articulate what I saw.

Over years of prayer, fasting, study, and divine guidance, I finally began to express a sliver of this revelation. The most vivid image was like a castle of cards. It was highly organized, complex, yet easy to destroy once its structure was understood. In these visions, I saw what I now call the circles of hell, the waves, and the systems used to distort and attack God's nature. Each part was intricate and deliberate. I prayed earnestly to do justice to what the Lord had shown me.

Map 1: The Chronological Evolution of Satan's Ministry

In this first map, we will explore what I call the Chronological Evolution of Satan's Ministry. Put simply, it is an overview of Satan's ongoing attempt to establish a parallel world: a counterfeit kingdom that imitates God's order and seeks to replace truth with lies.

This map traces his efforts from the moment of rebellion to numerous points in history where he tried to build his ministry and influence humanity.

This also reveals something crucial. Each time Satan fails, he repeats the same tactics. His strategies do not evolve; instead, they recycle. This proves not only his pride but also his insanity.

Therefore, the Holy Spirit led me to present this revelation in a historical framework, almost a prophetic timeline, so you can understand it both intellectually and spiritually.

I have divided this timeline into four spheres, distinct periods, during which Satan made major attempts to establish his ministry. Each sphere aligns with key biblical and historical events. While each sphere could be divided further, that is not what the Holy Spirit has asked me to do. For this purpose, I will focus on the four main eras, so we can clearly examine how the enemy's counterfeit kingdom has operated across history.

Time Sphere 1: The First Attempt — In Heaven

Time Period: From the Initial Rebellion to Satan's Fall
Location: Heaven
Focus: The Birth of Pride and the First Attempt to Create a Parallel World

Satan first attempted to establish his parallel world in Heaven, outside time and in eternity. In God's very presence, the seeds of rebellion were sown.

Jesus Himself gave us a glimpse into this event:

"He was a murderer from the beginning, not holding to the truth, for there is no truth in him. When he lies, he speaks his native language, for he is a liar and the father of lies" (John 8:44).

The root of all evil is pride. It is crucial not to confuse pride with arrogance, because they are not the same. Arrogance is a fruit—a visible, boastful behavior that others can observe. Pride, however, is the hidden root. It is a spiritual cancer that operates far beneath the surface.

Pride begins when wisdom becomes corrupted by self-focus. Wisdom is the profitable application of knowledge. **Pride is the destructive application of knowledge for a cause led by the self.** When a person looks too long at themselves instead of God, wisdom becomes distorted.

Lucifer gazed upon his own beauty and glory until it replaced his vision of the Creator. Pride is looking at yourself long enough to believe you are better than God or that you no longer need Him. Every fruit that grows from this seed can be traced back to pride, and one of those fruits is arrogance. Pride is not merely an emotion; it is a distortion of truth and a corruption of perspective. It is corrupted wisdom that leads to the action we call rebellion—going against God for the purpose of self. That action destroys.

We were created to behold God and to reflect His glory, not our own. Lucifer turned his gaze inward, and in doing so, he corrupted his purpose, his beauty, and his wisdom (Ezekiel 28:17). When truth was no longer directed toward God, it first died within him. From that internal corruption, deception was born, and what began in his heart soon expanded into open rebellion.

That rebellion did not remain private. Lucifer spread his lie outward and waged war in Heaven. Angels followed him in that rebellion. Scripture captures this moment with clarity:

"And another sign appeared in heaven: behold, a great, fiery red dragon having seven heads and ten horns... His tail drew a third of the stars of heaven and threw them to the earth" (Revelation 12:3–4)

This war, however, did not end in victory for him. His attempt to overthrow God and establish a counterfeit kingdom failed completely. Revelation tells us that war broke out in heaven, and Satan was rebuked, defeated, and cast out (Revelation 12:7–9). His first attempt to build a parallel kingdom—his first version of ministry—ended in total cosmic failure.

Lucifer cannot be forgiven because his rebellion occurred in eternity, outside of time. His choice was made in full knowledge, without limitation, and its consequence was final.

This moment marks the end of the first time sphere: the collapse of Satan's heavenly rebellion. From here begins the second time sphere. Having failed in Heaven, Satan attempted to rebuild what he lost—not above, but below. Not in Heaven, but in Eden. Not by creating, but by corrupting the very creation God had made.

Time Sphere 2 — The Second Attempt: Before the Flood

Time Period: From Satan's Fall to the Flood
Location: Eden and Earth
Focus: The Corruption of Humanity and the Counterfeit Image of God

After his defeat in Heaven, Satan sought another opportunity to build his parallel world, this time in Eden. He turned his attention to mankind in the garden, but also outside of the Garden on earth. Let's look at the Fall in Eden first.

Through deception, he invited Eve into his rebellion, speaking corrupted wisdom that mirrored his own fall.

"Now the serpent was more cunning than any beast of the field which the Lord God had made. And he said to the woman, "Has God indeed said, 'You shall not eat of every tree of the garden?" (Genesis 3:1).

By obeying Satan's voice instead of God's command, Adam and Eve submitted to Satan's rule voluntarily. Whoever you obey becomes your master. From that moment, authority and dominion were legally transferred to Satan.

This is explained in Romans 6:16, which says, *"Do you not know that to whom you present yourselves slaves to obey, you are that one's slaves whom you obey...?"* Through this legal transfer of authority, Satan gained access to the systems of the earth. Humanity, created to steward God's kingdom, became the vessel through which Satan attempted to build his counterfeit world.

Yet even in the midst of the Fall, the plan of redemption was already being revealed.

When God entered the Garden (Genesis 3:8–10), the broken state of humanity became instantly visible.

Adam and Eve hid, exposing their awareness of sin and the corruption now rooted in them. Shame, fear, and blame all sprang to life the moment they consumed the fruit.

Their actions immediately exposed the consequences of their disobedience. They hid from the presence of God (Genesis 3:8), something that had never existed before the Fall. Shame surfaced instantly, for suddenly they perceived themselves as naked (Genesis 3:7). This was the first evidence of spiritual corruption entering human nature.

God's questions were intentional and exposing: *"Who told you that you were naked? Have you eaten from the tree...?"*
(Genesis 3:11). He was not seeking information; He was revealing the truth now lodged in their hearts.

Adam blamed Eve (Genesis 3:12), Eve blamed the serpent (Genesis 3:13), and the integrity of human responsibility fractured on the spot.

Yet even in judgment, God hid redemption. He cursed the serpent (Genesis 3:14–15), but within that curse, He delivered the first prophecy of Christ. The *"seed of the woman"* would one day crush the serpent's head.

This was the earliest revelation of the Gospel, showing that God's plan of redemption existed before time itself.

God did not remove Adam and Eve from Eden as a cruel punishment but as an act of divine protection. Like a loving parent who disciplines for safety, His justice remained intertwined with mercy.

Their expulsion, specifically their removal from the Tree of Life (Genesis 3:22–24), prevented an eternal catastrophe.

If humanity had eaten from the Tree of Life while in a fallen state, they would have become eternally corrupt, locked forever in rebellion, just like Satan and the fallen angels. Sin committed in eternity cannot be redeemed.

So God placed mankind inside the boundaries of time. Time became the covering of mercy. Time made repentance possible. Time opened the path for salvation, restoration, and the coming of Christ.

This reveals a foundational truth: **Time itself is the substance of God's mercy.** Time and space became the environment where redemption could unfold.

Every moment, every breath, every delay is an extension of God's compassion stretched across time.

And this universe, this realm of time and space, is held together by the person of Jesus Christ. Scripture says He is the *"Exact representation of God's nature"* and that He *"upholds all things by the word of His power"* (Hebrews 1:3). He *"is before all things, and in Him all things hold together"* (Colossians 1:17). Time exists because Christ sustains it long enough for redemption to reach us.

This means that the laws of the cosmos, including time itself, are not independent forces. They are upheld by Christ in every moment. Time is mercy extended, held open by His hands.

The universe functions as a divinely appointed "space of repentance." God, who exists outside of time (2 Peter 3:8), created time as the stage of redemption. Its linear movement from past to future, life to death, judgment to eternity, is a merciful boundary preventing humanity's fallen condition from becoming eternal. By placing humanity within mortality, God created a window for salvation. Time allows us to repent, be transformed, and receive grace before judgment (Hebrews 9:27). Its very existence testifies to God's patience, *"not willing that any should perish, but that all should come to repentance"* (2 Peter 3:9).

When men began to multiply, and the corruption from their hearts was visible through their actions, Satan escalated his efforts. Scripture records a mysterious and catastrophic event that occurred before the flood, the union of fallen angels with human women. Genesis 6:1-4:

> *"And it came to pass, when men began to multiply on the face of the earth, and daughters were born unto them, that the sons of God saw the daughters of men that they were fair; and they took them wives of all which they chose... There were giants in the earth in those days... when the sons of God came in unto the daughters of men, and they bore children to them. The Nephilim were on the earth in those days and also afterward when the sons of God went to the daughters of humans and had children with them. They were the heroes of old, men of renown."* (Genesis 6:1-4)

The phrase "S*ons of God"* (Hebrew: *bene elohim*) is used in other parts of the Old Testament to refer to celestial or divine beings (e.g., Job 1:6, 2:1, 38:7). The New Testament book of Jude also references angels who *"did not keep their proper domain"* and are now held in chains for judgment, which many interpret as a reference to the event in Genesis 6. Ancient Jewish texts, like the Book of Enoch, explicitly name these *"Sons of God"* as angels called Watchers who descended to Earth to mate with human women.

So the sons of God (*bene elohim*) made children with the daughters of men. I believe that as they were corrupted under Satan, they extorted a new corrupted wisdom. All of it was brought forth with the intent to destroy humanity by completely cutting off the coming of Jesus by creating a satanic human: the Nephilim. The Nephilim would be incapable of carrying the plan of redemption, which is the seed of the woman.

The Nephilim were hybrid offspring, the result of a forbidden union between celestial beings and mortals. Satan's goal was to defile the image of God in mankind by introducing a counterfeit race, a hybrid creation that bore his rebellion in its very DNA.

You may ask, "If Satan created the Nephilim, does that mean Satan can create?" The answer is no. Satan does not possess creative power. What he does possess is access to the software of creation—reproduction, because of how he was originally designed. But that software still requires the womb of a woman. Satan did not create the reproductive system; he corrupted those who had authority to use it. He manipulated a divine process, but he did not originate it.

Scripture also emphasizes the condition of men in those days—they were evil! The lifespan of man was around five hundred years. The Bible mentions that God "regretted" creating man, but I do not believe God truly regretted man. I believe it was Jesus—the heart of God—expressing the deep sorrow of seeing creation fall away from divine purpose.

The Hebrew word used in Genesis 6:6 for regret is *nacham (נחם)*. While translated as "regret," "repent," or "was sorry," it is more nuanced than simple human regret. *Nacham* implies "to grieve," "to sigh," or "to be moved to pity".

In this context, God's *"regret"* expresses a profound, emotional sorrow over humanity's choices, rather than a miscalculation on His part. He was deeply pained by the widespread evil that had corrupted the very people He created in His image. This grief highlights God's personal and relational investment in creation, not a failure of His eternal plan.

To help us comprehend this, Scripture uses anthropomorphic language, attributing human characteristics or emotions to God, to help human beings picture and understand an infinite being. God doesn't have a physical heart in the human sense, but to say His "heart was deeply troubled" effectively conveys the depth of His grief over human sin. This is similar to how the Bible might describe God's *"strong right hand"*.

This is a literary device to make a spiritual truth more accessible. It's not a literal description of God's physical or emotional limitations, but rather a picture that can open your understanding. Each time anthropomorphism is used, it points to Jesus. The doctrine of God's immutability—that His nature and purpose are unchanging is affirmed in other parts of Scripture (Numbers 23:19; Malachi 3:6). There is no contradiction, but rather a distinction between God's unchanging nature and His dynamic relationship with creation through the picture of his son.

God's *"regret"* was not a change in His eternal plan for redemption but rather a moral and emotional response to humanity's changing actions. He remains faithful to His covenant while our experience of Him changes based on our choices. A holy and loving God must respond differently to obedience than to sin.

The life of Jesus further clarifies this grief. The Cross demonstrates the seriousness of sin—sin is so destructive that only the death of Christ could heal it. Ephesians 4:30 echoes the sorrow of Genesis 6, warning believers not to "grieve the Holy Spirit." Sin still wounds God's heart.

Yet even in Genesis, we see the same mercy displayed at Calvary. God provided Noah's ark as a means of salvation amid judgment, foreshadowing Christ, the ultimate Ark, who offers refuge to all who seek Him.

The presence of the hybrid Nephilim affected humanity. The depravity of mankind was under their influence, and I do not believe that the cosmos God created was made to support those spirits. Yes, they were present here through the authority Adam had ceded, but I believe that they were trespassing. Their presence triggered divine judgment.

God declared that His Spirit would no longer strive with mankind and set a limit of 120 years before the coming flood.

I believe that the essence of life in humans made their bodies able to sustain the hybrid life force. Let me be more explicit: I believe that the breath and the strength of God within us was the life force the fallen angels exploited to sustain their hybrid life.

Therefore, the hybrids were essentially living under our "breath." When God shortened the striving of His Spirit within mankind, it was again for our protection. Our bodies did not carry enough of the Spirit of God to continuously birth a race that would dominate us indefinitely.

This understanding is powerfully supported by the Hebrew meaning of Genesis 6:3, *"So the Lord said, 'My Spirit shall not strive with man forever, for he is indeed flesh; yet his days shall be one hundred and twenty years.'"* The Hebrew word for *"My Spirit"* is *ruach,* meaning My breath, My wind, or My life-force. This supports the revelation that divine breath sustains all life. The word translated as **"shall not strive"** (*lo-yadón*) carries a deeper meaning than mere contention. It implies not remaining, not dwelling, or not upholding permanently. God would no longer permit His *ruach* to be sustained endlessly in the current corrupted form. The use of **"forever"** (*le'olám*) signifies an eternal or timeless realm, confirming that mankind was rapidly moving away from a mortal capacity and towards a fixed, immortal (and corrupted) state. Finally, **"flesh"** (*basar*) denotes a mortal, limited, and corruptible being no longer spirit-sustained in an eternal capacity. The "120 years" establishes a divine limit on this access to the life-force, acting as a mercy boundary.

When God shortened the striving of His Spirit within mankind, it was again for our protection. This limitation of the spiritual life-force was essential to stop the transhuman corruption and prevent hybrid domination, as our human bodies could no longer effectively carry enough of the pure Spirit of God to sustain those beings indefinitely.

The flood was not solely a punishment. It can be seen as a natural response within the divine design to Satan's attempt. Recall that he was overthrown in various realms and throughout different ages. The flood served as a purification of creation. Satan attempted to create a parallel world, which ultimately failed and is destined to fail. The flood was a divine reset intended to preserve the original lineage from which the Messiah would eventually come.

I had a revelation the other day when I read about Noah's ark. The flood lasted 40 days. This reminded me of every 40-day fast in the Bible, giving me a deep revelation! When you fast for 40 days, the flood happens in your bloodline. All the **Nephilim** in your DNA go under a flood because heaven opens its window. I pray that from this passage in the book, you get excited, to fast and pray.

When the Nephilim, these giant hybrid beings, perished in the Flood, their human nature died with their physical bodies. However, their angelic component did not simply disappear. Many ancient Jewish and early Christian traditions teach that because they were neither fully human nor fully angelic, their spirits were left bound to the earth, disembodied and restless. Unable to return to Heaven and without physical bodies to inhabit, they became antagonistic toward humanity, roaming as hostile spiritual entities seeking embodiment and influence.

These disembodied spirits of the Nephilim are referred to as demons or evil spirits. They became restless entities searching the earth for bodies to inhabit. *"When an unclean spirit goes out of a man, he goes through dry places, seeking rest, and finds none"* (Matthew 12:43). The remaining spirits of the Nephilim are sometimes considered among the lowest ranks of the fallen: spiritually unauthorized, disembodied, and constantly seeking embodiment.

Time Sphere 3 — The Third Attempt: After the Flood

Time Period: From the Flood to the Crucifixion
Location: Earth
Focus: Dominion Through Kingdoms, Idolatry, and Counterfeit Rule

After the Flood, Satan shifted his strategy from corrupting human DNA to corrupting human systems. If he could not destroy the lineage of the Messiah biologically, then he would attempt to dominate humanity politically, spiritually, and culturally. Thus began the rise of empires under his influence. Kings, rulers, and emperors became instruments through which he sought dominion.

But even as Satan organized nations under darkness, God was already preparing the covenant that would bring forth Jesus Christ. Satan's systems grew, but they could not outmaneuver God's mercy.

This age marks Satan's move from biological corruption to governmental control. He abandoned the strategy of giants and instead focused on shaping kingdoms, establishing false religions, and mimicking God's covenant structure. He created counterfeit priesthoods, false prophets, and entire religions built on deception. This was the rise of *systemic darkness*—a political and spiritual imitation of God's order.

From Babel to Rome, we see a sequence of world systems designed to imitate God's order without His holiness. At Babel, humanity united under one language and one ambition — not to glorify God, but to "make a name for themselves." The Tower of Babel was an engineering marvel, a revelation of human ingenuity that set the stage for further advancement in later time spheres, including our own.

But these discoveries were aimed at reaching heaven without holiness. Humanity attempted to build a gateway to eternity without the prerequisite of transformation. This is arrogance. This same pursuit remains today as science often disguises its rebellion as research meant to "elevate humanity." Massive investments are poured into exploring star-gates, space colonization, or unlocking metaphysical realms — not to honor God, but to escape Him. Repentance and holiness would be far simpler, but that requires surrendering the worship of human intellect.

Quantum physics, metaphysics, cosmology, anthropology, psychology—none of these defile the existence or the ruling of God; they confirm it. Every time you use a discovery to try to "cheat" God, you reveal the most Satanic infection in your heart. You have time in this life to repent and return, rather than trying to rush into eternity broken, open, and stuck outside of the presence of God forever. Your discoveries do not belong to you! They existed in their integrity before the mercy of God opened your eyes to them. The reason you discover them is that they reveal more of God. The thing you discover did not start existing the moment your eyes opened upon it.

"Come, let us build ourselves a city and a tower whose top is in the heavens; let us make a name for ourselves..." (Genesis 11:4).

In this time period, all fundamental false religions gained territory through the land, appointed by the people. Through the authority of these rulers, Satan shaped the world with his ideology, and we were introduced to a new corrupted wisdom called division. The one thing all those kingdoms had in common, whether great or small, was that they were for themselves. They all saw themselves as the greatest. They carried a distorted version of "truth" shaped by their own perception, a truth born from the same desire that defines Satan: the urge to expand, to dominate, to rule over others, and to claim more territory.

I am not saying that all kings, emperors, or rulers were inspired only by corruption and Satan. We see God's mercy shown through His appointed men and women of God, such as David, Joseph, and Esther. Satan was doing his best, but God's will was unbothered.

Nations practiced idolatry by worshiping the fallen ones who presented themselves as gods. Behind every idol from every kingdom stood a spiritual entity, a fallen angel. The names changed to Baal, Moloch, Ra, Zeus, and Diana, but the spirit behind was the same. Each demanded sacrifice, loyalty, and worship, just as Satan's ministry operated. Through idolatry, Satan built a false priesthood. He built a counterfeit of Father Satan himself. He had his prophets, his altars, his rituals.

Some empires that rose under Satan carried a demonic assignment; for example, Babylon represented rebellion and confusion. Egypt embodied bondage and the worship of creation instead of the Creator. Assyria carried cruelty and domination. Greece exalted knowledge above truth. Rome enforced power and control through violence and human glory. It seems as if he was creating his body on earth.

Yet every time Satan built his structure, God responded with redemption. God is always a few steps ahead. God called Abraham, through whom He would establish a covenant, not an empire. Through Abraham, God introduced His own kingdom order on Earth. Then came Israel, a nation born not of conquest but of promise. Through the Law, the Prophets, and the Temple, God revealed His original design for a holy people, distinct from the nations ruled by darkness.

And at the fullness of time, Jesus entered the scene as the Son of God. In only three years of ministry, Jesus made Satan's entire establishment of world government collapse entirely.

"Having disarmed principalities and powers, He made a public spectacle of them, triumphing over them in it" (Colossians 2:15).

Time Sphere 4 — Satan's Ministry After the New Covenant

Time Period: From the Blood of Jesus to the End of Time
Location: The Earth, the Church, and the Nations
Focus: Deception, infiltration, and confusion to take people away from the light.

The New Covenant destroyed the ordinances of darkness and broke the dominion of evil. Yet the residue of sin within human nature, what I call the DNA of the Fall, must still be diligently confronted and destroyed by each believer. Think of it this way: a sickness can be cured, and medication can be prescribed, but the sick person must take it manually. In the same way, the blood of Jesus paid for the sin of Adam and Eve (and by extension, for all humanity), but its power must be personally applied to each of us through faith and obedience.

You might ask, "If Jesus already won, why does Satan's ministry still exist? Why does darkness still operate?" The answer is simple: Satan was overthrown, his authority sealed, and his end declared. However, the victory of Jesus must be applied intentionally and personally in your life. The Bible gives us the tools to do this. Satan can no longer operate with legal authority because his dominion was stripped by the blood of Jesus. Yet he still functions through deception. Deception is power borrowed from ignorance.

In this era, Jesus Himself revealed Satan's ongoing strategy. Jesus showed us that He was always several steps ahead. He told us plainly that many false Christs and false prophets would arise. Therefore, there is no need for shock or surprise. The true danger is not in how shocking evil appears, but in how oblivious believers can become. Scripture reveals these things not to frighten us, but to prepare, protect, and guide us.

Satan still uses the same ancient tools: deception, corruption, lies, and the twisting of truth. But today the Kingdom of Heaven has been publicly revealed for your access, the blood of Jesus has been shed for your redemption, and the Word of God has been written for your instruction.

We are no longer in an age of ignorance. We have been given every resource necessary for victory: the Word, the Spirit, the blood, the name, and the full revelation of Christ. Failing without access is one thing; failing with full access is rebellion in the heart. A person who remains in bondage despite having freedom within reach is resisting the very grace offered to them. This rebellion leads to separation from God.

Jesus defined Satan's final strategy as the rise and operation of the Antichrist. Satan has always wanted to be Christ. He craves worship, rulership, and the loyalty that belongs only to the Son. The Antichrist is his final attempt to establish a counterfeit Christ. The Greek word ἀντίχριστος *(antikhristos)* itself reveals the nature of this deception. Anti does not only mean "against"; it also means "instead of" or "in place of." It describes a rival presence, one that resists Christ while attempting to imitate Him. *Christos* means *"The Anointed One,"* the Messiah. Together, the term Antichrist describes the spirit of Satan in the last days, opposing Christ by pretending to be Him.

Jesus Himself described the movement of the Antichrist spirit long before John ever used the word. He revealed it through function and fruit, warning us that *"false Christs and false prophets will appear and perform great signs and wonders to deceive, if possible, even the elect"* (Matthew 24:24). In this warning, Jesus exposes a new level of deception, one that is performative. It does not simply lie; it *displays*. It performs. It seeks to impress you with signs so it can gain access to your trust, and through your trust, access to your dominion.

The Greek reveals the weight of Jesus' warning. The verb used is *dōsin*, meaning "to produce, to show, to give" a deliberate demonstration of supernatural activity. These acts are called *sēmeia* (signs carrying symbolic meaning) and *terata* (wonders that evoke amazement). Scripture often uses these terms to describe divine acts, but here they are performed with a deceptive motive. Their purpose is captured in the Greek verb *planaisai*, "to lead astray, to deceive, to cause to wander." Jesus is not describing random trickery; He is exposing intentional spiritual strategies designed to mislead.

When Jesus says they will "perform great signs and wonders," He is warning us that these signs will manifest with a purpose crafted to appear meaningful, crafted to stir emotion, crafted to appear divine. This is why I often call it "prophetic circus," "the upside-down red cross," or "appreciation worship," where the performance becomes the message, and people are robbed of the time they should spend with God.

The combination of *sēmeia* and *terata* shows two levels of deception: symbolic deception and emotional deception. The signs communicate a false truth; the wonders capture your attention long enough to draw you into agreement. And Jesus says plainly that this deception will be so convincing that even the *eklektoi*, the *elect God's chosen*, those set apart for His purposes, would almost be deceived if it were possible. It means the deception will resemble truth so closely that only those anchored in Christ's voice will withstand it.

Lack of knowledge and understanding is the doorway through which this deception enters. When a person trusts a false prophet or any entity shaped by iniquity, they unknowingly submit their dominion. Trust is the bridge to your will, and once your will is compromised, your authority follows. This principle is written into the law of life and death; choose one, and the fruit will follow (Deuteronomy 30:19).

This is why Jesus spoke so clearly. The goal of these warnings was recognition. The spirit of the Antichrist must be recognized in daily life. Christianity is not shaped by emotion or personal interpretation. It is defined by the One who established it. Christ is not who you feel He is. He is who He says He is.

The Apostle John then expands on Jesus' warning, giving us the clearest definition of the spirit behind these false signs. He alone uses the word *antichristos* in Scripture, and he reveals its operation in what he calls *"the last hour."* He shows us that the Antichrist is both coming as a final figure and already present as a spirit, a system, and a mindset working through people. Many assume the

Antichrist is only a false prophet on a platform, but you do not need a stage to operate in that spirit. You do not even need to know Christ personally to oppose Him or try to imitate Him.

John writes, *"Children, it is the last hour; and as you have heard that the Antichrist is coming, even now many antichrists have come."* He reminds us that, unlike previous generations, we are not spiritually blind. We have heard, we have been warned, and we stand accountable for the truth we know. Then he exposes the core identity of the Antichrist spirit:

"Who is the liar? It is whoever denies that Jesus is the Christ. Such a person is the Antichrist, denying the Father and the Son" (1 John 2:22).

This denial is not a one-time refusal. The Greek phrase *ho arnoumenos hoti Iesous ouk estin ho Christos* refers to one who continually rejects the identity of Jesus. *Arneomai* means to disown, refuse, or reject alignment with truth. *Christos* refers to the divinely appointed Messiah. To deny Jesus in His true identity is to deny the Father Himself, for the Son cannot be separated from the Father. This ancient deception, wrapped in modern language, is the same spirit whispering the lie spoken in Eden: *"You shall be as gods."* It tells you that you can shape truth apart from the One who is Truth Himself.

This separation, this desire for the moral influence of Jesus without His Lordship, has become the signature of the spirit of the Antichrist in our generation. It appears everywhere people admire His teachings yet resist His authority, reinterpret His divinity, or reshape His identity to fit their preferences. It is rebellion disguised as enlightenment. It is the denial of Christ hidden beneath the vocabulary of spirituality.

And this is exactly what we see echoed across countless belief systems today: honoring Jesus as wise, but not as Lord; respecting

Him as teacher, but denying Him as Christ; accepting His words, but rejecting His blood. Outward acknowledgement with inward denial. It is the very pulse of the Antichrist spirit moving through culture, religion, and philosophy, ancient rebellion repackaged for a modern world.

Let us examine some of those religious beliefs that follow the pattern of acknowledging Jesus outwardly, yet inwardly denying the fullness of who He is.

Islam acknowledges Jesus ('Isa) only as a prophet or messenger, but explicitly denies His divinity, His crucifixion, and His resurrection. The Qur'an declares, *"They did not kill Him, nor crucify Him; it was made to appear so" (Qur'an 4:157)*. This means the redemptive act that defines salvation in Christianity is completely denied.

Judaism, in its mainstream form, also rejects Jesus as the Messiah and refuses to acknowledge Him as the Son of God. It holds to the Talmudic expectation that *"the Messiah has not yet come."*

Jehovah's Witnesses claim that Jesus is God's Son but teach that He was the first created being, and therefore not co-eternal or equal with the Father. This is the same ancient Arian heresy the early church condemned.

Mormonism (The Church of Jesus Christ of Latter-day Saints) teaches that the Father, the Son, and the Holy Spirit are three separate gods. They are "one" only in purpose, not in essence. Their theology even states that God the Father was once a mortal man who became divine. It is taught within Mormonism that faithful humans can also become gods through "eternal progression," a direct denial of Jesus' uncreated and unique divinity.

Ahmadiyya Islam goes further by asserting that Jesus did not die on the cross. Instead, He was taken down alive, recovered, and died later in India. Mirza Ghulam Ahmad, their founder, wrote, *"Jesus did not die on the cross."* This statement removes the very foundation of atonement.

In the New Age movement, Jesus is portrayed as one of many "Ascended Masters," an enlightened being who achieved "Christ consciousness." This idea teaches that "Christ" is a universal state of awareness anyone can reach, completely separating the divine title from the person of Jesus. The popular *"A Course in Miracles"* even claims, "Christ is a state of awareness within you." These statements deny Jesus as the exclusive mediator between humanity and God.

Similarly, many who identify as "spiritual but not religious" say, "I believe in Jesus, but not religion." They treat Jesus as a wise moral teacher while rejecting His divinity, His blood atonement, and His authority as Lord.

Hinduism often honors Jesus as a holy man, avatar, or incarnation of Vishnu, but views Him as one among many divine manifestations. The Hindu saying, *"Truth is one, the wise call it by many names,"* expresses a belief that all paths lead to the same truth. This directly opposes Jesus' own declaration that He is *"the way, the truth, and the life"* (John 14:6).

Buddhism respects Jesus as a compassionate teacher, sometimes calling Him a bodhisattva, but holds firmly that *"no one saves us but ourselves."* Thus, it rejects the necessity of divine atonement.

Modern theological trends show the same spirit. Deconstructive Christianity and Progressive Christianity openly reinterpret or discard core doctrines such as Jesus' divinity, His authority, and His atoning death. Deconstruction often mirrors the spiritual path of Masonic initiation. It begins with questioning and ends in relativism and denial. Progressive voices like Richard Rohr teach that *"Jesus reveals God's love, not God's judgment."* He redefines the cross as metaphorical and the resurrection as symbolic. This turns salvation from an objective act of grace into a subjective feeling or evolution of consciousness.

Non-Trinitarian groups, such as Unitarians, reject the deity of Christ entirely. They teach that Jesus was a great moral reformer but not divine. Universalism asserts that all people will be saved regardless of faith or repentance, undermining the very purpose of Christ's sacrifice.

Syncretistic Christianity, mixing Christ with voodoo, ancestral worship, or other spiritual practices, equates Jesus with local spirits or ancestors. *"Jesus and the ancestors both protect us"* is a common teachings that diminish His unique Lordship.

The Prosperity Gospel redefines the cross into a message of wealth and comfort, proclaiming that *"faith is a force; prosperity is your right."* This is in opposition to the redemptive suffering of the Savior.

Sikhism regards Jesus as a holy teacher but not the divine Son of God, stating that *"all prophets are equal messengers of the One."*

The Bahá'í Faith likewise honors Jesus as one of several *"Manifestations of God,"* but denies His unique divine person and exclusive atoning role. Instead, they teach that "Jesus was divine, but so were Muhammad and Bahá'u'lláh."

All these systems, though different in appearance, share one spiritual root: **the denial or distortion of the true identity of Jesus Christ.** They strip Him of His exclusivity, diminish His divinity, or reinterpret His sacrifice. This is precisely what Scripture identifies as one of the purposes, operations, and characteristics of the spirit of antichrist. Any teaching that denies, by definition, "Jesus is the Christ" (1 John 2:22) is the spirit of antichrist. Whether through open rejection or subtle redefinition, these beliefs stand in opposition to the Gospel's truth that salvation is found in Christ alone. For this reason, no matter how moral, mystical, or intellectual they appear, they should not be followed. To accept them is to step away from the Light of Christ into deception.

In 1 John 4:3, we find even greater clarity about the character of the spirit of the Antichrist: *"Every spirit that does not confess that Jesus Christ has come in the flesh is not from God. This is the spirit of the antichrist."* The word *confess* is deeper than a simple verbal "yes." To confess means to fully see, believe, acknowledge, and align yourself with the truth of who Christ is. Truth must move from understanding to confession to action. If a body cannot fully confess and publicly acknowledge that Jesus has come in the flesh, then that spirit is of the Antichrist.

The Greek text reinforces this. *Pan pneuma ho ou homologei Iēsoun Christon en sarki elēlythota* means every spirit that refuses to *homologei* to say the same thing God says, to agree with His testimony openly, is not from God. This confession is not optional; there is no salvation without alignment. *En sarki elēlythota*, "has come in the flesh," is written in the perfect tense, announcing both the historical incarnation and the continuous reality that Jesus remains fully human. Any spirit that rejects this truth is false. And many still wrestle with this right now. Spiritual warfare begins with becoming a Christian, and a Christian stands upon the non-negotiable truth of who Christ is. If you cannot come into agreement with Jesus' testimony, you will remain outside, vulnerable to the seduction of the Antichrist spirit.

A false prophet is anyone speaking against the truth of Jesus, denying the integrity of God, or leading others into corrupted wisdom. Just as Christ does not live only inside a building, the Antichrist spirit does not operate only inside a church. Christ sustains the universe, and this false spirit tries to imitate Him in the shadows.

Paul, Peter, and Jude together unveil the remaining anatomy of this spirit. Paul calls it *to mystērion tēs anomias, "the mystery of lawlessness,"* revealing a rebellion that uses the language of God without the submission of the heart. He calls this figure *"the man of lawlessness" and "the son of perdition"* (2 Thessalonians 2:3). This lawlessness is a return to self, a deeper descent into selfishness, a spirituality without truth. When Paul says that this mystery is *"already at work,"* he is exposing that this force is not waiting for the end; it is already functioning wherever people reject God's government, yet keep His vocabulary. And the fact that Paul unmasks it shows that its defeat is guaranteed.

Peter warns that this spirit rises first, not outside the Church, but *within* it. False teachers appear "among you," introducing destructive heresies that deny the Master who bought them (2 Peter 2:1). The verb *arnoumenoi* describes a deliberate, continuous internal contradiction—following God's structure while rejecting His nature. It is rebellion disguised as devotion, truth mixed with error, until holiness is reduced to convenience.

Jude completes the exposure: they turn grace into *aselgeia*, a license for immorality. This is the most seductive form of the Antichrist spirit: grace without transformation, forgiveness without repentance, love without holiness, liberty without accountability. It promises freedom while chaining the soul to corruption. This counterfeit grace is one of Satan's final deceptions.

Through the writings of the apostles, the schemes of the enemy are fully unmasked. They show us that the Antichrist spirit is already judged and overthrown at the Cross.

Christ disarmed the powers of darkness (Colossians 2:15) and declared their end. And yet, though defeated, this spirit still roams the edges of time, searching for agreement from anyone living outside submission to truth. We now live in what I call the fourth time-sphere, a suspended realm of divine mercy where God still extends grace to mankind. But this mercy will not stretch forever.

When the limits of mercy close, time and space will collapse into the moment of judgment, and eternity will begin.

Even so, the apostles teach that the spirit of Antichrist, though active, is already defeated. The victory is eternal, but humanity stands in the tension between two kingdoms: the kingdom of darkness that has already fallen, and the kingdom of Christ that is about to be fully revealed. Through revelation, I have come to believe that Satan is bound to repeat the same fall in the realm of time that he suffered in eternity. It is recorded in the stars and the seasons as his punishment. It is shown to you as a gift of redemption, a map to overcome. From the lens of fear and confusion, it may seem like Satan refined his strategy across time, but when you look closely, you see he did not. He cannot. His rebellion happened outside of time, and it was final. His nature is fixed. Your final form, however, is defined by how close you choose to draw to God during your time here. Satan has no time to change, but you do.

We are witnessing the manifestation of his fall replaying itself, not for his benefit but for your victory. And that replay is a gift. You either overcome him by the blood of the Lamb and the word of your testimony, or you mirror his nature, his traits, and his fall. Even if you choose wrongly, each new morning brings renewed mercy, a fresh invitation to stand in the eternal victory of Jesus. This is only the beginning of what God desires to show you.

The ministry of Satan is real, but it is also fully defeated and diminishing. His time is collapsing. His influence is shrinking. And every revelation of truth brings you deeper into the triumph that Christ secured. The victory is already written; your role now is simply to walk in it.

Chapter 3 — It's Time To Surrender Your Parallel World And Walk Into Your Path of Destiny

I'm sure that you must feel overwhelmed by all that you've learned in the previous chapters. Maybe you've heard this information before, though I strongly doubt it. Before we continue into deeper revelation, I would like to lead you into a prayer. This book is not for you to identify Satan in your neighbor, your mother, your boss, or your husband. This book is meant to open your eyes to the schemes you've fallen for, the realities you've embraced, and the pursuits you've formed out of a lack of knowledge.

It's time to pray. It's time to repent, return, and renounce your parallel world. What is a parallel world? It is when you mimic Satan's rebellion and pride, using his tools—deception and witchcraft—in your time and actions to create the world you want. It's when you do this despite God's calling, destiny, instructions, and direction for you.

Knowingly or unknowingly, you cannot walk in your true destiny while trying to build your parallel world. Spiritual warfare is renouncing Satan and destroying the parallel world he inspired us to build so that he could gain territory under your breath. It is choosing to walk in the true path of destiny God has ordained for us.

Prayer of Renunciation: Tearing Down the Parallel World

Father, in the name of Jesus, I come before you with an open heart, fully aware that, knowingly or unknowingly, I have helped build and sustain a parallel world, a counterfeit reality patterned after Satan's rebellion. I confess that through pride, fear, desire for control, or the wounds of rejection, I have agreed with the enemy's blueprint. I have built my own version of Eden, my own throne, my own truth, my own way. I have established altars of self-will and crowned my own logic as king. Forgive me, Lord.

Today, I renounce every system, pattern, or mindset that has mirrored the rebellion of Satan. I renounce the need to be my own god or to create my own truth, kingdom, or righteousness. I renounce every false structure that gave Satan access to my dominion, identity, or imagination. Every counterfeit world I've built in my thoughts, relationships, emotions, or pursuits, I tear down now by the authority of Jesus Christ.

Father, I confess I entertained lies that appeared as light. I trusted voices that promised power but produced bondage. I followed desires that looked divine but were rooted in deception. Today, I break every covenant with the false kingdom I participated in. Let the blood of Jesus dissolve every code, altar, and connection that tied me to darkness—visible or invisible.

I reject every form of false wisdom, every imitation of the Spirit, and every pursuit of knowledge apart from You. I reject counterfeit purpose, peace, love, and revelation. I dismantle the structures of pride, comparison, competition, lust, manipulation, control, rebellion, and fear. I command the ruins of my parallel world to crumble under the weight of Your truth.

Father, I return to your original design. I surrender my dominion back to You, the rightful King. Let the Word become the foundation of my new reality. Let Your Spirit fill every space that was once occupied by deception. I lay down my crown, agenda, and ideology. I receive the mind of Christ in their place.

From this moment forward, I decree that my spirit will no longer serve as a portal for darkness but as a dwelling place for glory. My thoughts will no longer host rebellion but revelation. My imagination will no longer reproduce hell's images but heaven's blueprints.

Father, purify the atmosphere in my home, relationships, calling, and mind. I renounce the counterfeit reality and embrace the divine order of Your Kingdom. Let heaven invade my soul. Let Your truth be my compass. Let Your presence become my environment.

Today, I choose deliverance over delusion. I choose obedience over opinion. I choose surrender over self. I am no longer a co-builder with rebellion; I am a co-heir with Christ. **In the name of Jesus Christ, the One who conquered the rebellion and crushed the serpent, I am free, I am redeemed, and I am restored to divine order. Amen.**

We have renounced the *"parallel world"* inspired by Satan's schemes. Now, let us accept the invitation to walk into the path of destiny God has designed and predestined for us. You might ask, "Why are we talking about destiny in the middle of a spiritual warfare book?" It is because the Holy Spirit has led me here. I am not following my own literature's logic or structure. I know this is a point where Satan's confusion reigns, so it makes perfect sense to address it now.

To know what destiny is is not enough. The goal is to accept it and actively walk in it. A lot of people tell me, "I know what my destiny is," but they are incapable of taking the steps to get there. They treat destiny like a final destination on a map, forgetting the journey. If what you "know" doesn't move you to action, do you actually know enough? What if you know it in *perception* but don't know it in *truth*? This means you don't know it with Jesus in the equation. When Jesus is integrated into the knowing part of any information, He brings an automatic movement, an attack on complacency.

With that being said, what exactly is destiny? The word *"destiny"* has many definitions. The one we are focusing on is the theological definition of destiny. Destiny is the divine plan or purpose that God has established for an individual, a people, or creation as a whole. It is attached to three non-negotiable principles: God's sovereignty, predestination, and your free will.

God's Sovereignty is His supreme control over the universe and everything within it. He is in charge of the big picture, the timeline, and the very fabric of existence. You don't control the foundation of the world; He does. *"My own hand laid the foundations of the earth, and my right hand spread out the heavens; when I summoned them, they all stood up together"*(Isaiah 48:13). We must submit to the fact that God is the author and finisher of the plan.

Predestination is not a rigid fate that removes choice; it is God's proposal. It is His preparation, and His powerful invitation. He initiated the plan long before you took your first breath. *"Before I formed you in the womb, I knew you [and approved of you as My chosen instrument], and before you were born I consecrated you [to Myself as My own]; I have appointed you as a prophet to the nations"* (Jeremiah 1:5). God's destiny for you is already a finished work in the spiritual realm. The path is set, the calling is clear, and the tools are provided.

Free will is where you come in. Free will is your freedom to engage with God's invitation or to reject it. God will never force His destiny upon you. He has already secured the victory through Christ, but you must choose to walk in that finished work each time. You have the authority to choose the "parallel world" inspired by Satan, or the path of destiny inspired by God.

"I call heaven and earth as witnesses against you today, that I have set before you life and death, the blessing and the curse; therefore, you shall choose life so that you may live, you and your descendants" (Deuteronomy 30:19).

Your choice determines your outcome. Spiritual warfare is about consistently choosing life and destiny over death and your self-made parallel world.

A *"path"* is simply defined as the course or direction in which a person moves, or the specific course of action or conduct they choose to follow. In the spiritual realm, these paths are not neutral. There are only two fundamental paths in life, and they define your eternal outcome:

The Path of Destiny: The specific course God has ordained for your life, aligned with His divine plan and purpose.

The Paths of Destruction: The broad way the devil ordains, which actively leads you away from God's perfect plan and towards death and self-destruction.

There is a choice we have to make between these two sets of roads. Jesus Himself made it very clear that the choice is binary; there is no middle ground or third option. In Matthew 7:13-14, Jesus said, *"Enter through the narrow gate. For wide is the gate and broad is the road that leads to destruction, and many enter through it. But small is the gate and narrow is the road that leads to life, and only a few find it."*

This *"broad road"* literally means wide, spacious, or roomy. So a different set of destructive choices, all spilling, charming, and seductive, is bigger. In contrast, the narrow gate or the path of destiny is tight, restricted, and requires intentionality, sacrifice, and submission to God. This path can only be engaged in with Jesus as the lead. Choosing a path is a significant decision. The path of destiny is when you accept and choose to walk in the specific, predestined direction that God proposes and invites you into. Each choice comes with an invitation. Each time you accept it, you establish a step on your path. Those steps are designed for the life God has for you. You are walking *through* Him. You are walking with him. Did you know that path has a name? Its name is **Jesus**. He is not just a guide on the path; He *is* the path itself.

"Jesus said to him, 'I am the [only] Way [to God] and the [real] Truth and the [real] Life; no one comes to the Father but through Me'" (John 14:6).

This literally means he is God's self-existent presence on earth. He is the only road to the Father. He embodied all truth. He is the source of eternal life. No one can reach God the Father except through him.

When I started this chapter, I gave you the theological definition of the word "destiny." In the Bible, *"destiny"* is also associated with the translation of the term "appointed time." Destiny is not a final destination. It is the perfect confirmation through those appointed times of your walk in your path of destiny.

What this means is simple: when you walk in Jesus, you don't miss any of your divinely appointed times. You are aligned with God's timeline, staying inside the stretch of His mercy. You resist the devil at each opportunity, not based on feeling, but based on the knowledge of who God is. God operates on a divine calendar. The Bible says that time and seasons are recorded in the stars. Your ability to not miss any of your appointed times (*kairos* moments) set in eternity *is* the definition of being in your destiny.

Genesis 18:14 says, *"Is anything too hard or too wonderful for the Lord? At the appointed time, when the season [for her delivery] comes around, I will return to you, and Sarah shall have borne a son."* Just as God had an exact appointed time for Isaac to be born, He has specific, non-negotiable times for your breakthrough, ministry, healing, and marriage. The path of destiny ensures that you are positioned in the right place, at the right time, for those moments of divine manifestation.

Furthermore, walking in His path means we operate with a clear conscience and an absolute trust in His ultimate judgment and timing. We stop judging situations or people prematurely, knowing that God is the righteous judge and will reveal all things in His appointed season. This concept is laid out by the Apostle Paul.

"My conscience is clear, but that does not make me innocent. It is the Lord who judges me. Therefore, judge nothing before the appointed time; wait until the Lord comes. He will bring to light what is hidden in darkness and will expose the motives of the heart. At that time, each will receive their praise from God" (1 Corinthians 4:4-8).

The path of destiny is fundamentally a life of alignment, trust, and readiness. It ensures that we step into every single divine appointment prepared and precisely on time.

Some people think *"destiny"* is a final destination or a place where they are rewarded, pleased, and full of what they desire. That is not destiny. That is the desire to fulfill your *"parallel world."* Jesus taught us to *"seek first the kingdom of God, and everything else will be added."* Some of you actually hate the destiny that God assigned to you and want to direct your own steps. You put a label called Jesus on your self-made plan. When you truly renew your mind, accept the integrity of things, and renounce the devil, it is easier to accept the truth. You have nothing in your eyes, mind, or heart that rejects it.

If you have gotten to this section of the book and still think, *"yes, my path of destiny is taking me to a place where I will be successful,"* it is advisable to go back. Read this book from page one again. You did not design your path. If you cannot fall in love with your path immediately, please go on a fast to re-evaluate yourself. Detoxify yourself from the destructive desires you have and renounce the corruptive wisdom you have gained. This chapter may reveal a new layer of witchcraft and control in you that you have to let go of.

Everyone wants to know what their final self will be, even when the Bible clearly reveals the goal. The enemy has created these obsessions for the future to rush you and make you choose any broad road that comes your way. But Satan also creates this sense that you have all the time in the world to choose God. Do not be fooled. The path is a path; you do not decide how fast or how slow you go. Your job is to abide in Him because the knowledge of your future is not going to assure you that you will make it there the way you are supposed to.

Knowing the final destination in iniquity, without investing in the path with the one who created the path for you, will not assure that you will arrive at the final destination your soul truly craves. You can know who you are supposed to marry, but if you do not get ready on the path, you will reject the person and delay your life. Seeking first the Kingdom means getting the transformation and the training along the way. Every divine appointment becomes a graduation for the next step before the next appointed time. I have to confess, it was impossible for me to truly fall in love with the destiny God had for me, the man God had for me, the calling God had for me, without first understanding the integrity of all these aspects. It required me to actively let go—through deliberate action —of my own self-constructed destiny. Now, I am completely in love with where Jesus is taking me.

But where is Jesus taking you? Jesus is taking you back to your original place—the dwelling place of glory. Jesus is taking you to the ultimate appointed moment outside of time: the Wedding Feast of the Lamb. He illustrates this beautifully in Matthew 22. The parable perfectly illustrates the section we just covered. The story is about a King who invites guests to His Son's wedding, but they refuse the invitation. They treat it with contempt and focus on their own affairs, including their farms and businesses (the *"parallel world"* discussed earlier).

> *"Jesus spoke to them again in parables, saying, "The kingdom of heaven may be compared to a king who gave a wedding feast for his son. And he sent his servants to call those who had previously been invited to the wedding feast, but they refused to come. [...] But they paid no attention [they disregarded the invitation, treating it with contempt] and went away, one to his farm, another to his business.[...] Then he said to his servants, 'The wedding [feast] is ready, but those who were invited were not worthy. So go to the main highways that lead out of the city, and invite as many people to the wedding feast as you find.' Those servants went out into the streets and gathered together all the people they could find, both bad and good; so the wedding hall was filled with dinner guests [sitting at the banquet table]."* — Matthew 22:1-10

Jesus goes on to say that when the King came in, he saw a man without wedding clothes. When questioned, the man had no excuse. The King ordered him to be tied up and thrown into the outer darkness, where there would be weeping and grinding of teeth. Jesus concludes the parable by saying, *"For many are called [invited, summoned], but few are chosen."* You can find the full text of this section of the parable in Matthew 22:11-14.

These two scriptural images (Matthew 22 and Revelation 19) clearly show our final destination is not defined by our temporary beauty or glory here on earth, but rather by the eternal event of the wedding feast itself. The angel in Revelation 19:9 confirms the blessedness of this invitation: *"Then the angel said to me, 'Write,*

'Blessed are those who are invited to the marriage supper of the Lamb." And he said to me [further], 'These are the true and exact words of God.'"

Our path on Earth is our preparation for this eternal moment. The ultimate destiny is to enter a state of perpetual worship to the Father and give to him the glory he deserves. This destination is beyond the constraints of our current time-sphere and our earthly lives. It is a moment of pure, unhindered worship. Here, we lay down our earthly *"crowns"* and acknowledge the Creator in His fullness:

"Whenever the living creatures give glory, honor, and thanks to him who sits on the throne and who lives for ever and ever, the twenty-four elders fall down before him who sits on the throne and worship him who lives for ever and ever. They lay their crowns before the throne and say: 'You are worthy, our Lord and God, to receive glory and honor and power, for you created all things, and by your will they were created and have their being.'" — Revelation 4: 9-11

The path of destiny takes you from your self-made parallel world of pride and temporary satisfaction back to your original place of intended glory, participation, and eternal worship at the Marriage Supper of the Lamb.

Section V

Demonology 101

Chapter 1 — The Stars That Fell With Him

Welcome to Demonology 101. The purpose of this chapter is to discover the nature, origin, and hierarchy of demons, beginning with the biblical account of their fall, just as I did with Satan in Section 3 of this book. This is an origin study. We will identify who fell, what Scripture means when it calls them *"stars,"* how the fall happened, and what that rebellion produced in the spiritual realm. By starting at the beginning, we remove confusion, replace assumptions with Scripture, and establish a clear foundation for everything that follows.

Revelation 12:4 — *The Stars and the Dragon "And his tail swept across the sky and dragged away a third of the stars of heaven and flung them to the earth. And the dragon stood in front of the woman who was about to give birth, so that when she gave birth, he might devour her child."*

Many readers overlook a crucial detail in the book of Revelation: demonic beings are first identified as *"stars,"* a biblical term used to describe angelic beings. Revelation 12:4 makes it clear that Satan—depicted as the great dragon—did not fall alone. He dragged a third of the stars from heaven and cast them to the earth. In a single verse, Scripture reveals both their celestial origin and their former identity as part of God's heavenly order.

A closer look at the Greek language of Revelation 12:4 deepens our understanding of how this fall unfolded. The phrase καὶ ἡ οὐρά αὐτοῦ (*"and his tail"*) does more than describe a physical feature. It points to a hidden strategy. The tail represents Satan's indirect influence—his ability to manipulate from behind the scenes when he could no longer confront the throne of God face to face.

The verb συρεῖ / ἔσυρεν, translated as *"dragged"* or *"swept,"* conveys forceful movement. It describes pulling, drawing, or carrying along with power. The imagery is that of a violent current, a spiritual riptide strong enough to sweep away those who yielded to its pull. This was not a gentle following; it was a forceful removal driven by deception and influence. The phrase τὸ τρίτον τῶν ἄστρων τοῦ οὐρανοῦ—"a third of the stars of heaven"—confirms that these were not physical stars, but heavenly beings. In apocalyptic language, stars consistently represent angels, and here they are shown falling under Satan's deception.

The text then states that he *"threw them down to the earth"* (καὶ ἔβαλεν αὐτὰ εἰς τὴν γῆν). The verb ἔβαλεν is decisive and violent. It means to hurl, cast, or expel with force. These beings were not merely relocated; they were ejected, stripped of their position, and cast out under judgment. What Scripture reveals is not a gradual descent, but a forceful expulsion—a decisive act that severed them from their place within God's heavenly order and marked the irreversible nature of their fall.

To understand **who the stars are**, we must allow Scripture to interpret itself. If you recall Section 3, Chapter 3 of this book, we examined Satan's access by studying how he was created and by exploring the choirs of angels. That foundation now becomes essential. The question before us is not abstract or symbolic; it is precise and structural: *what is the spiritual identity of the "stars" mentioned in Revelation, and from which ranks did they fall?*

To establish a framework, we begin with Psalm 19:1–2: *"The heavens declare the glory of God; and the firmament sheweth his handiwork."* This passage shows the stars actively *displaying* God's works. That action is not poetic imagery alone; it describes function. The stars are presented as participants in manifesting and maintaining God's order within creation. This leads us to ask which angelic choir is responsible for *"shewing"* God's handiwork?

Traditional angelology points to the Virtues (also referred to as Powers). These angels are often called the *"shining ones"* and are associated with governing the elements, maintaining natural order, and overseeing the visible operations of creation. They are frequently described as being involved in the workings of miracles related to the physical universe. This role aligns directly with the Psalm's description of the heavens declaring God's glory through what is seen and governed.

By cross-referencing the function attributed to the stars in Psalm 19 with the established roles of the angelic choirs, we begin to identify their original rank and hierarchy. Now that we have established this framework, we can apply the same method to the stars mentioned in Revelation 12:4.

The first clue appears in Revelation 1:20, where Jesus Himself defines the term: *"The seven stars are the angels of the seven churches."* In this verse, the stars are not only identified as angels, but they are also shown operating with a specific function and assignment. These angels are entrusted with oversight connected to churches—earthly institutions operating within time, history, and human affairs. When this function is cross-examined with the established angelic hierarchy, it aligns with angels assigned to direct engagement with humanity.

The second clue is also found in Revelation 1:20, which uses the same noun root for "stars." Revelation 1:20 uses ἀστέρες (asteres), while Revelation 12:4 uses ἀστέρων (asterōn), meaning "of the stars." Although the grammatical form shifts from singular to plural, the word itself remains the same. This confirms that Scripture is referring to the same category of beings.

Because the same term is used in both passages, it clarifies that the stars swept from heaven in Revelation 12:4 are the same angels identified by Jesus in Revelation 1:20.

Therefore, the stars that fell with Satan were angels assigned to earth-facing governance—primarily from the Third Sphere, with influence extending into the lower Second Sphere.

The prophet Daniel was given a vision that mirrors what is revealed in Revelation 12:4, and we know this because both passages describe the same core event: a celestial rebellion in which heavenly beings are cast down from their appointed place. Revelation shows the action through symbolic imagery—the dragon sweeping a third of the stars from heaven—while Daniel provides a parallel vision that adds structural detail. In Daniel 8:10, he records, *"It grew great, up to the host of heaven. And some of the host and some of the stars cast down to the earth."* The use of the same imagery—stars being cast down—confirms that Daniel and John are witnessing the same fall from two prophetic angles.

What distinguishes Daniel's account is his use of the word *host*. In the ancient Hebrew context, the word *tsābā' (host)* is an organized army operating under hierarchy and command. By separating "some of the host" from "some of the stars," The host points to higher organizational ranks within the heavenly system.

When this distinction is cross-examined with the established choirs of angels, the reference to "some of the host" indicates that Satan's influence did not stop at the front-line ranks. It reached upward into the lower levels of the Second Sphere, affecting beings such as Powers and Virtues, who were entrusted with governing systems, natural order, and cosmic function.

When the passages describing the fall are examined together, a consistent pattern emerges. Scripture records the fall of angels described as *stars* and as part of the *host of heaven*, yet none of these accounts identify any angelic beings from the First Sphere as participants in the rebellion. The biblical testimony is notable not only for what it reveals, but also for what it withholds. While Satan himself—identified elsewhere as a former Cherub—turned away from the Light, there is no scriptural evidence that the Seraphim, the Cherubim as a class, or the Thrones followed him in rebellion.

The rebellion, therefore, did not overtake heaven entirely. It reached a clear and immovable boundary. The First Sphere remained untouched. The beings closest to God's throne—those whose existence is defined by direct proximity to His presence—were not persuaded, not deceived, and not displaced. Scripture consistently presents these orders as remaining in their appointed place before God, reinforcing the conclusion that the fall was limited in scope and rank.

The conclusion is that Satan did not fall with the highest order of heaven. He fell with a structured portion of the angelic hierarchy— primarily angels of the Third Sphere, with influence extending into the lower Second Sphere. Daniel reveals ranks. Revelation reveals consequences. Together, they testify that the hierarchy of the stars that fell with him were never equal to the authority or order of God.

The first stream consists of fallen angels—described in Scripture as "one-third" of the stars and only "some" of the host. The resulting kingdom of darkness is therefore organized, not because darkness itself creates order, but because of how these beings were created before they were violently swept away by Satan's tail. They continue to function within structures and hierarchies in heavenly places. These beings retained rank, memory, and system-level knowledge. They operate through territories, governments, cultures, and institutions, influencing the world from positions that mirror the order they once served. Their rebellion did not erase their understanding of structure; it corrupted it.

Chapter 2 — The Structure of Darkness

The Apostle Paul regroups and clarifies the entire understanding of demonic hierarchy. When we read Ephesians 6:10–12, his framework is the result of revelation, scholarship, and spiritual discernment. He was a trained intellectual, a teacher of the Gospel, and a witness to divine truth.

His contribution is decisive because he does what Scripture consistently does when dealing with spiritual realities: he classifies them. He names ranks, jurisdictions, and spheres of operation. By doing so, he gives us a system map of the kingdom of darkness: **principalities, powers, rulers of darkness, and spiritual wickedness in heavenly places.**

This structure directly confirms the framework established in the previous chapter. Chapter 1 traced who fell from which ranks and within what limits. Paul now shows us how those fallen beings continue to operate. He does not contradict the origin story; he organizes its outcome. What Revelation shows as an event outside of time, Paul presents as an ongoing system in time and space.

When the Holy Spirit led me to lay the foundation of this study, I was directed to use Paul as both confirmation and conclusion. His writings provide the clearest apostolic framework for understanding how fallen angels are arranged and how they exert influence within the world. Through careful study and extended time with the Holy Spirit, it becomes evident that apostolic revelation carries an internal logic.

This chapter, therefore, answers a necessary question: *What is the structure of darkness?*

Paul writes: *"Finally, my brethren, be strong in the Lord, and in the power of his might. Put on the whole armour of God, that ye may be able to stand against the wiles of the devil. For we wrestle not against flesh and blood, but against principalities, against powers, against the rulers of the darkness of this world, against spiritual wickedness in high places"* (Ephesians 6:10–12).

First, Paul names **Principalities** (The Territorial Architects)
Origin: Third Sphere (Earth-Facing/National Governance)

Original Assignment: They were the **Divine Regents** over the nations. Their role was to steward specific people groups and territories, guiding them toward their unique redemptive purposes and ensuring the harmonious development of diverse human cultures.

Corrupted Assignment: They now act as **Territorial Strongholds**. They pervert *"stewardship"* into *"ownership,"* binding land and people through regional cycles of sin, ancestral trauma, and the spiritual fortification of borders against the Gospel.

Second, Paul identifies **Powers** (The Systemic Enforcers)
Origin: Second Sphere (Administrative/Structural Governance)

Original Assignment: They were the **Managers of Divine Order.** Their role was to oversee the mechanisms of authority and the flow of administration throughout creation, ensuring that all created systems (laws, physics, and social functions) operated in alignment with God's throne.

Corrupted Assignment: They now act as **Institutional Tyrants.** They infiltrate the structures of human society—governments, legal systems, and economic engines—to enforce corruption, systemic injustice, and "spiritual red tape" that blocks the manifestation of God's kingdom.

Third, Paul refers to the Rulers of the Darkness of this World (The Ideological Governors)
Origin: Second Sphere (Atmospheric/Global Influence)

Original Assignment: They were the **Keepers of Light.** Their role was to distribute divine wisdom and moral clarity throughout the cosmos, acting as filters that ensured the "light of God's glory" was translated into understandable truths for all creation.

Corrupted Assignment: They now act as **Cosmic Blind-folders.** They specialize in "conditioning the atmosphere." Rather than attacking individuals, they shape the "Spirit of the Age" by engineering false ideologies, cultural norms, and global entertainment that make darkness appear as light and truth appear as foolishness.

Finally, Paul names Spiritual Wickedness in High Places (The Strategic Saboteurs)
Origin: Heavenly Places (Spiritual Command & Control)

Original Assignment: They were the **Ministers of Divine Alignment**. Their role was to facilitate the synergy between heaven and earth, coordinating the timing of divine interventions and maintaining the purity of the spiritual atmosphere closest to God's presence.

Corrupted Assignment: They now act as **Strategic Obstructors.** Operating from the highest vantage point, they do not fight over dirt (territory) or systems (powers); they fight over *timing and revelation.* They specialize in blocking prayers, disrupting the *"sending"* of the Church, and launching strategic assaults to prevent divine breakthroughs from reaching the earth.

This category must not be confused with *evil spirits,* also called *unclean spirits,* which are a separate and distinct class.

Unclean spirits are *earthbound.* They do not operate through rank, jurisdiction, or heavenly authority. Instead, they function through proximity to humanity and direct attachment to individuals.

Their origin is tied to the corruption described in Genesis 6, where fallen angels from the lower ranks abandoned their proper domain. The hybrid beings produced through that transgression were destroyed, but their spirits were left disembodied. These spirits now wander the earth, seeking embodiment.

Chapter 3 — To Steal, To Kill, To Destroy (The Weapons Fashioned Against You)

When we study the weapons fashioned against us, we do so exclusively in the light of Christ. This study provokes awareness. In the Kingdom of God, awareness is the precursor to wisdom, and wisdom is the foundation of spiritual strategy and the development of discernment.

Scripture issues a persistent call to this heightened state of perception, a disciplined way of living. The Bible establishes this awareness through three specific spiritual postures, each designed to keep the believer alert, grounded, and aligned with truth.

The first is **prudence—wisdom and discernment**. *"The wisdom of the prudent is to understand his path"* (Proverbs 14:8). Prudence is the refusal of moral blindness. It is the ability to look beyond the surface of a situation and discern the long-term consequences of a choice before taking a step. Prudence guards against being misled by folly and trains the mind to recognize direction, outcome, and intent. It is a spiritual skill—being practiced in perceiving one's steps so that decisions are made in alignment with truth rather than impulse.

The second is **vigilance and alertness**, the watchfulness of a sentinel. *"Be sober-minded, be alert; because your adversary the devil prowls around like a roaring lion"* (1 Peter 5:8). Vigilance is the refusal of spiritual passivity. Like a sentry positioned at a gate, the alert believer remains attentive to subtle compromises that seek access to the soul. This watchfulness is not rooted in fear, but in responsibility. To be alert means we are prepared to respond—not only to threats, but also to the divine opportunities God places before us. Vigilance keeps the heart awake, the mind engaged, and the spirit ready to discern both danger and direction.

The third is **intellectual and spiritual clarity**, the posture of the strategist. *"So that Satan may not outthink us; for we are not ignorant of his schemes"* (2 Corinthians 2:11). To be sober-minded is to maintain a mind free from the intoxicants of emotional turmoil and worldly distortion. This clarity keeps perception sharp and judgment steady. By remaining sober-minded, we prevent the enemy from outmaneuvering us. We move from being ignorant of his methods to being fully aware of his patterns, able to recognize repetition, anticipate strategy, and respond with truth rather than reaction.

The outcome of this disciplined awareness is spiritual sensitivity. It is cultivated through submission to God's authority (James 4:7) and through the renewing of the mind (Romans 12:2). When we live in this posture, our perception is sharpened, and our inner senses are trained. We become able to discern the voice of God amid the noise of the world, to identify a scheme before it manifests in the natural realm, and to execute strategy with responses that are timely, wise, and compassionate rather than reactive or driven by fear.

We must remain aware of both the condition and the nature of God's protection. God's protection is described in Scripture as the heritage of the servants of the Lord. The Bible speaks openly about the devices of Satan, not to frighten believers, but to keep them alert. God exposes these strategies so His people are not surprised by attack, but equipped to recognize and resist it.

Let's pause for a minute and talk about an extremely crucial detail that is constantly brushed off: the fact that God's promises are conditional. God's promises are released when you follow the conditions He sets for them. God can't release a promise outside of His order and protection. His protection involves you fulfilling your condition. As you fulfill it, you become able to cherish and sustain that promise without leaving God out of the center. This is the same for His protection in Isaiah 54:17 and many other verses. It specifies that the weapons fashioned against you are not prospering because of your alignment, which is the fulfillment of the condition attached to that promise.

That covenant standing is called *"servant of the Lord"* in this specific verse. I have met so many believers who believe—without a foundation of truth—that the devil's weapons can't work in their lives because of the work they do *for* God. In reality, they are not doing this work *with* God. What they do for God is by their own standards, and sometimes what they produce is the fruit of iniquity.

They believe that the weapons that are formed against them do not prosper because of their worldly status and worldly interpretation of success. You being praised by people is not on the list of requirements for the weapon to not prosper. They think they are so important that they can be above the law of the Spirit that God Himself follows.

Many believe the love of God is a blanket of absolution that removes all consequences and repercussions for their actions; however, this is a dangerous, false belief that treats mercy as a free pass for lawlessness, and to think that way is to align your mind with the logic of Satan.

The eternal law remains: the wages of sin are death. Legally, sin demands the shedding of blood—this is why the Cross is the only answer. While Jesus paid that debt in full on the Cross, covering us all, many still find the enemy's weapons prospering in their lives. This is not because the Blood has lost its power; it is because they have placed themselves in the realm of death, curses, and bondage. When you step out of God's order (disobedience), you enter the territory where the devil is legally free to steal, kill, and destroy despite the Blood that is accessible to you.

Surrendering your free will to ignorance is equivalent to granting Satan a license to operate in your life. Many people falsely believe that the enemy's weapons are failing simply because they have a *"Christian"* sticker on their car or a copy of Psalm 91 on their refrigerator.

If you believe you are untouchable simply because you *"deserve"* protection, repent. Protection is a reward of alignment. Inheritance is a result of placement. The simple fact that you do not understand that God's protection is based on your proximity to His presence and your capacity to obey His conditions is proof that the weapons are prospering right now. They have been prospering for a long time, hidden behind the veil of your own spiritual negligence.

Let's look at some spiritual warfare verses in the Bible that describe God's protection and require a certain position from you.

Psalm 91 — Linguistic Anatomy of Protection

POSITION — "He who dwells in the secret place of the Most High."

The Hebrew verb used for *dwells* is יָשַׁב *(yāshab)*. This word means *to sit down, to remain, to settle, to take up residence*. It does not describe movement, visitation, or emergency access. It describes permanence. To *yāshab* is to live positioned under authority, not to approach God only when danger appears.

The phrase *secret place* comes from the Hebrew סֵתֶר *(sēter)*, meaning *a concealed space, a covering, a place hidden by protection*. This is not secrecy through distance, but protection through proximity. The position described is one of alignment — a life settled under God's rule, order, and authority.

RESULTING PROMISE — *"No evil shall befall you."*

The Hebrew words used for *fear* and *evil* in this passage refer to calamity that overtakes, terror that dominates, and harm that gains control. The promise is not that danger does not exist, but that it does not gain access.

RESULTING PROMISE — *Angelic Protection*

The text states that angels are *commanded* concerning you. The Hebrew structure implies assignment, not occasional intervention. They are sent to guard you *in all your ways*—meaning the ordered paths of obedience you walk in, not paths outside alignment.

RESULTING PROMISE — *Divine Presence*

God declares, *"I will be with him in trouble."* The Hebrew construction emphasizes presence, not removal. The promise is not the absence of trouble, but the absence of abandonment during trouble. Protection flows from position. Presence flows from dwelling.

Isaiah 54:17 — Linguistic Anatomy of Covenant Protection

POSITION — "This is the heritage of the servants of the Lord, and their righteousness is of Me."

The Hebrew word for heritage is נַחֲלָה (naḥălāh). It means an inherited possession, a legal allotment, something assigned by right, not earned by effort. A heritage is not something you strive to obtain; it is something you receive because you belong.

The word *servants* comes from עֶבֶד (ʿebed), meaning *one who belongs to a master by covenant*. This is not forced submission; it is relational alignment. A servant in this sense operates under protection, provision, and authority because they remain under their master's covering.

The phrase *"their righteousness is of Me"* uses the Hebrew צְדָקָה *(ṣĕdāqāh)* in this context. This does not mean moral perfection. It means *right-standing, legal alignment, covenant positioning.* This righteousness is not produced by human effort; it is granted by God. The position described is one of alignment with God's covenant identity, where condemnation, shame, and self-righteousness lose legal ground.

RESULTING PROMISE — *"No weapon formed against you shall prosper."*

The Hebrew verb for *formed* indicates intention and craftsmanship. The weapon is real. It is designed. It is aimed. But *prosper* in Hebrew carries the meaning *to advance, to succeed, to break through with effectiveness.* The promise is not that the weapon will not exist, but that it will not accomplish its objective.

RESULTING PROMISE — *"Every tongue that rises against you in judgment you shall condemn."*

The word *tongue* here refers to accusation, legal speech, false testimony, and spiritual indictment. To *condemn* means to declare invalid, to render powerless, to strip of authority. This is not emotional retaliation; it is legal authority exercised from a position.

RESULTING PROMISE — *Vindication*

The text concludes with divine authorship: *"This is from Me."* Vindication does not come from self-defense. It comes from God acting as judge, witness, and defender on behalf of those who remain in position.

Matthew 16:18 — Linguistic Anatomy of the Living Stone

POSITION — *"Upon this rock I will build my church."*

The word *rock* Jesus uses here is πέτρα *(petra)*, not *petros* (a small stone), but *bedrock*, a massive, immovable foundation. This rock is not Peter himself as a man, but the revelation Peter just confessed—that Jesus is the Christ, the Son of the living God. Position, therefore, is not personality or effort; it is placement upon revealed truth. The word *build* comes from οἰκοδομέω *(oikodomeō)*, meaning *to construct a house with intentional structure, order, and permanence.* God is not assembling something fragile. He is building something designed to last.

The word *church* is ἐκκλησία *(ekklēsia)*. It does not mean a building or a gathering alone. It means *those who are called out and assembled under authority for a purpose.* The church is not a crowd; it is a structured body placed under Christ's headship.

Peter later explains this same truth in 1 Peter 2:4–5, using the phrase λίθοι ζῶντες *(lithoi zōntes)*—*living stones.* A living stone is not an independent material. It is shaped, positioned, and fitted into a larger structure. To be a Living Stone means you are not self-supporting; you are sustained by connection. You do not define your place; God assigns it.

To live as a Living Stone is to be built into Christ's structure, not to live spiritually detached. You are not your own. You are placed, positioned, and joined to the spiritual house through revelations of who Christ is.

RESULTING PROMISE — *"The gates of hell shall not prevail against it."*

The word *gates* comes from πύλαι *(pylai)*, which refers not to weapons but to defensive structures, governing entry points, and authority centers. Gates represent jurisdiction, strategy, and control —not attack. *Hell* here is ᾅδης *(Hadēs)*, the realm of death, corruption, and separation from God. And *prevail* comes from κατισχύω *(katischyō)*, meaning to overpower, dominate, or gain superiority.

The promise is not that hell will not resist us; rather, the promise is that hell will not overpower, penetrate, or dismantle what God is actively building. Because you are part of a divinely structured house, the strategies of darkness simply cannot break you, enter you, or collapse you. The reason for this is found in the nature of engagement: gates do not advance; they merely attempt to hold their ground. Christ declares that even the strongest defensive systems of darkness cannot withstand the pressure of what He builds.

Yes, there are diverse weapons fashioned against us, and we are about to review them. However, before breaking down those weapons, it is necessary to establish a foundational truth—a formula of light: **God's promises are conditional**. This single reality dismantles ten thousand weapons fashioned against you. This is what is revealed when we look at darkness through the lens of light. It is a specific revelation that hell does not want you to see or engage with. Position matters. Hell needs you to be positioned in its gates in order to prevail.

Now, moving from accepting this reality to walking in the right position requires steps. Following God's prescriptions in Scripture takes time. This is why God gives mercy and leaders from the five-fold. Growth, alignment, and maturity do not happen instantly; they unfold as we submit to His order. Some may grit their teeth at this revelation, but that resistance may reveal something deeper. It may expose an infection of pride in the heart. God's promises are, in fact, conditional—not as punishment, but for protection, growth, and development.

A blessing received before its appointed time **becomes a curse**. Not because God's gift is evil, but because it is received outside of God's order and preparation. God's plans are to prosper us and not to harm us, and therefore His promises and His timing are inseparable.

Jeremiah 29:11: *"For I know the plans I have for you,"* declares the LORD, *"plans to prosper you and not to harm you, plans to give you hope and a future."*

When desire reaches ahead of preparation, pride replaces trust. What was meant to bless begins to expose immaturity, self-reliance, and misalignment with God's process.

These conditions are not burdens to perform; they are truths to be learned and applied; they transform and fortify. Promises of protection, breakthrough, and destiny function within divine order. Christianity itself is a position. Being a **Christian is not merely a belief system; it is a belief system emerging from a believer's position, a divine status one is invited into by God's mercy.** There is more deliverance found in being correctly positioned in the light than in fighting darkness while standing outside the position of power.

The Diversity of Weapons

The diversity of weapons used by Satan does not imply that he is inventive. I used to think the kingdom of darkness was an artistic place, and the Kingdom of God was boring. I am not the only one who believed that. The weapons are not as numerous as they appear. I have a theory that Satan repeats himself because he is bound to do so. His defeat in every realm of time is a part of his judgment.

The diversity of tactics used does not imply they are original. It's often thought that complex strategies are always creative, but sometimes the most effective approaches are simply variations on core themes. While diverse in their application, these tactics can often be traced back to a limited number of fundamental strategies.

If we look carefully, the manifestation of these tactics can vary greatly depending on the context and the target. One way to conceptualize this is that underlying intentions can result in a wide variety of outcomes tailored to different situations. We can understand these tactics through a layered approach:

Layer 1: At the Core (Fundamental Objectives)

At the core of every tactic, weapon, and deception used by the enemy lies a single, unchanging agenda. Scripture defines it plainly in John 10:10. His work against humanity is carried out through three fundamental actions, each serving a deeper and more sinister purpose: the establishment of dominion through the consumption of human life.

The enemy seeks to live beneath the very breath God placed within humanity. He feeds on what was meant to glorify God—our spiritual vitality, identity, and divine potential—and uses it as material to build his counterfeit kingdom. Every act of theft, violence, and destruction is aimed at expanding this twisted, parallel world over human lives.

To Steal *(klépsē)*. This word means to take something secretly, deceitfully, and without the owner's knowledge or consent. Spiritually, it describes the theft of truth, peace, joy, identity, and security in Christ. The enemy rarely begins with open destruction; he begins by quietly removing what anchors a person to God, often without immediate detection.

To Kill *(thýsē)*. This term does not describe ordinary murder. It carries sacrificial and ritual implications. The enemy does not merely seek to end life; he seeks to use people as offerings for his own gain. He aims to extinguish Christ within the believer—to silence divine life, purpose, and presence—turning what was meant for worship into fuel for his rebellion.

To Destroy *(apolésē)*. This word conveys total ruin: to abolish, devastate, render useless, and erase hope entirely. It describes spiritual annihilation—a condition where connection to God is severed and replaced by bondage to darkness. Destruction is the final stage, where identity is erased, purpose is collapsed, and the soul is left desolate; yet tethered to the enemy instead of God.

Together, these three objectives form the foundation of every strategy Satan employs, a systematic process designed to consume life.

Layer 2: Building Blocks (Core Strategies)

Scripture does not present evil as something that appears fully formed; it is built. The Bible consistently reveals sin, deception, and bondage as a process of construction. Jesus spoke of houses being entered, occupied, and fortified (Matthew 12:43–45). Paul described strongholds as structures erected in the mind (2 Corinthians 10:4–5). James outlined desire giving birth to sin, and sin growing until it produces death (James 1:14–15). In the same way, a physical building requires materials.

Darkness prepares the ground. Lies lay the framework. Hatred hardens the structure. Witchcraft seals agreements. Bondage reinforces walls. Curses extend the structure through generations. Strongholds complete the fortress. These are called building blocks because each one supports the next. Remove one, and the structure weakens. Expose the order, and the construction collapses. These core strategies are the methods through which Satan implements his objectives—stealing, killing, and destroying—using our spiritual lifeblood as the material to construct his walls. If Layer 1 reveals what the enemy wants, Layer 2 reveals how he builds it.

Darkness promotes the absence of light, truth, awareness, and discernment. It produces the inability to think critically or spiritually perceive. This is moral and spiritual obscurity—an environment where divine truth is suppressed, and confusion becomes normal. Darkness creates the condition of chaos that allows Satan's kingdom to expand quietly and efficiently.

Lies promote falsehood and establish paths designed to lead people away from God and closer to death. A lie distorts reality, redirects allegiance, and reshapes belief. Every lie is intentional, guiding the soul further from truth and deeper into agreement with darkness.

Hatred promotes, guides, and invites further evil influence. It is the pursuit of life fueled by hostility, where love is diminished and replaced by bitterness. Hatred becomes Satan's substance within the core of a person, producing moral aversion and spiritual separation from a life anchored in God.

Witchcraft acts to seal a contract into a bloodline. Through sorcery, manipulation, drugs, or occult practices, a person attempts to create a personal or parallel reality. In truth, this action transfers dominion. What appears to be empowerment is surrender—participation in Satan's system in exchange for a false reward. The individual aligns with his way, and Satan receives legal access to their authority.

Bondage is the result of the contract. It is the band that tightens around the soul, producing despair and compelling repeated agreements with darkness. Each time a person sins to cover a wound instead of healing it, spiritual blood is shed. That blood is not wasted. It is used as material to build walls—across timelines and bloodlines—resulting in slavery and spiritual imprisonment under a cruel master.

Curses are the visible outcome of bondage and contract extended through generations. A curse is an imprecation, a malediction—the opposite of a blessing. It manifests as recurring patterns of spiritual, emotional, or physical struggle rooted in sin, rebellion, or occult involvement. What was once a personal agreement becomes a generational inheritance.

Strongholds are the final manifestation of becoming a "dead stone" for Satan. They are fortifications—places of strength—constructed within the mind and soul. Figuratively, they are entrenched thought patterns, arguments, and high-minded ideas that oppose the knowledge of God. These barriers are not physical structures, but internal strongpoints that resist truth and maintain agreement with lies, curses, bondage, and darkness.

Together, these building blocks explain how the enemy moves from intention to occupation. What begins as darkness becomes a system. What starts with a lie ends in a fortified fortress.

Layer 3: Specific Tactics (Individual Actions or Methods)

These are the *moment-by-moment* attacks Satan uses to accomplish his core objectives. They are "tailor-made" assaults, applied at precise moments in time to exploit immediate vulnerabilities, as illustrated in Luke 22:31. While Layer 1 defines the enemy's unchanging goals and Layer 2 exposes the building blocks he uses to construct bondage, Layer 3 reveals how those strategies are executed in real life—through specific, timely actions.

Arrows / Fiery Darts: These are sudden, intense, and precisely aimed attacks. They manifest as spikes of fear, anxiety, acute temptation, or sharp accusations. Unlike long-term oppression, arrows are immediate strikes meant to destabilize faith in the moment. Their goal is not endurance, but shock.

Scripture often describes these attacks as occurring "by day," meaning they strike during active, conscious moments of life—when decisions are being made, words are spoken, and direction is chosen.

"Thou shalt not be afraid for the terror by night; nor for the arrow that flieth by day..." (Psalm 91:5–6)
"Above all, taking the shield of faith, wherewith ye shall be able to quench all the fiery darts of the wicked." (Ephesians 6:16–17)

"Who whet their tongue like a sword, and bend their bows to shoot their arrows... suddenly do they shoot at him." (Psalm 64:3–4)

These attacks are quenched by faith applied immediately.

Snares / Traps: Snares are deceptive setups designed to capture a person through carelessness, fatigue, or unguarded moments. Unlike arrows, snares are hidden. They only work when the target is unaware. Once triggered, they produce restraint and entanglement, often leading to patterns of bondage.

Scripture describes these traps as devices of the *"fowler"*— carefully laid and intentionally concealed.

"Surely he shall deliver thee from the snare of the fowler..." (Psalm 91:3)

"Our soul is escaped as a bird out of the snare of the fowlers..." (Psalm 124:7–8)

"That they may recover themselves out of the snare of the devil..." (2 Timothy 2:26)

Snares often follow agreement. Awareness and truth are the means of escape.

Serpents & Scorpions: These represent specific expressions of demonic power that operate through venom rather than immediate destruction. They manifest as toxic influences, persistent irritations, spiritual harassment, or sharp pains—emotional, physical, or psychological—designed to distract and intimidate rather than kill outright.

Jesus identifies these tactics explicitly and then immediately establishes the believer's authority over them.

"I give unto you power to tread on serpents and scorpions, and over all the power of the enemy..." (Luke 10:19–20)

"...they shall take up serpents; and if they drink any deadly thing, it shall not hurt them..." (Mark 16:17)

These tactics lose their effect when authority is exercised. Authority is the outward evidence that comes from a believer's boldness when they live from their position.

Darkness / Pestilence / Destruction: These forces operate collectively and often invisibly. They are permitted during seasons of chaos, crisis, or judgment and are designed to overwhelm environments rather than individuals. Their goal is to produce despair, confusion, and the perception that God has withdrawn His protection.

"Nor for the pestilence that walketh in darkness; nor for the destruction that wasteth at noonday..." (Psalm 91:6–7)

"He disappointeth the devices of the crafty..." (Job 5:12)

These tactics depend on the atmosphere. They lose power when God's covering is recognized, trusted, and obeyed.

Strongholds (Individual Manifestation): While strongholds are established through the strategies outlined in Layer 2, they become active tactics when a person repeatedly agrees with a lie and refuses to dismantle it. At this stage, the stronghold is no longer theoretical; it becomes operational.

"Casting down imaginations, and every high thing that exalteth itself against the knowledge of God..." (2 Corinthians 10:4–5)

"Neither give place to the devil." (Ephesians 4:27)

A stronghold is sustained not by Satan's power, but by human agreement and recollection—agreement sustained through constant engagement in imagination. When truth is applied during meditation on the word of God in renewing the mind, the structure collapses.

Identification of the Crack in Your Foundation

Identifying the cracks in your foundation is synonymous with deliverance from the weapons, tactics, and objectives of hell that have been taking advantage of the negligence you have allowed yourself to be in. Awareness is amazing. Coming back to your senses is powerful beyond what we can sometimes imagine. We have talked about diverse weapons. Let's now expand on this chapter and discuss the significant agreements you participate in that sustain those weapons: the cracks in your foundation.

There are two primary cracks in your foundation:

The crack you are born with (our inherited human nature and previous family bondage).

The crack you continually create (through your own negligence).

You might say, "I didn't know I had to fix cracks!" You get saved, and Jesus provides the tools to prevent you from creating more cracks. He also gives you the tools to fix all the existing ones so that people after you can live on a solid foundation. The goal of Christianity is to become a blessing, a repairer of the bridge, an extension of Jesus' mission. To complete this mission, the cracks in your foundation need to be repaired.

A crack in your foundation is not the same as a test. Life comes with many challenges and tests, sometimes wrongly perceived as attacks. But before any breakthrough or advancement, a test must come. Those tests are checkpoints so we can continue building our foundation on Jesus alone. That solid foundation is a list of presets and concepts Jesus directed to help you cycle through life successfully. It ensures that when the storms of life come, or the scream of the devil blows, your house will stand firm.

Let me remind you that the Church is a spiritual house built on collective, living stones. Jesus declared that the gates of hell will not prevail against His Church (Matthew 16:18). If you are not a living stone, the gates of hell will prevail over you. And if the gates of hell prevail over you, you will become an instrument of hell. The question is: Are you a living stone, or are you a dead stone?

I love this image of a stone because that is where the revelation of the crack came from, and it is linked to the word "foothold." A "crack" is the defect, and a "foothold" is how it is used. The crack is the structural weakness in your foundation. The enemy identifies that crack and puts his "foot" in it to gain a stable position, which is the foothold. Once a foothold is gained, the enemy has the leverage needed to implement his core strategies [Layer 2: lies, darkness, bondage, etc]. A foothold is a smaller, initial point of entry that, if neglected, can develop into a "stronghold" (a fortified structure or mindset). You must fill the crack and remove the foothold to restore the structure's integrity.

How do we identify a crack in our life? This is based on your behaviours and traits. More precisely, it is based on how you respond to things and to God over time. **The fruit of the Spirit is the result of the Holy Spirit within you; the works of the flesh are the result of a foothold in those cracks.** When you are led and progressively obey the spirit of the living God, as a result of a position, He deals with every crack.

Identifying the Cracks and the Manifestation of the Flesh

The evidence of a cracked foundation is found in the "*works of the flesh*" (Galatians 5:19-21). When these behaviors are present, confusion and demonic activity are often nearby (James 3:14–16). These behaviors are the visible manifestation of unseen internal cracks and spiritual vulnerabilities that serve as footholds for the enemy.

Some of the most common cracks the enemy exploits are **insecurity, comparison, and selfish desire**. The manifestation (works of the flesh) of these internal cracks would be **jealousy, envy, and pride.** The *result* of these behaviors in action is exactly what Jesus identified as the enemy's agenda: **to steal, kill, and destroy.**

From Crack to Foothold to Stronghold

You can be born with a crack, but if neglected, they provide the leverage (foothold) the enemy needs to establish a fortified stronghold.

1. Insecurity: The Foundation Crack

Insecurity is often a *"generational fracture,"* a fragility you may have been born with or developed through early trauma. It is a fundamental lack of trust in who God is, and consequently, who He says you are. This crack exists because your identity is not anchored in the "*Rock*" of Christ.

Insecurity becomes a foothold when you begin seeking external validation to fill the internal void. When you give people, performance, or possessions the power to define you, you give the enemy a seat at the table of your identity.

The Stronghold of insecurity, if left unchecked, can mature into a **Spirit of Fear**. You become a prisoner to the "*fear of man*," where your life is no longer led by the Holy Spirit, but by the desperate need to please others or avoid rejection.

2. Comparison: The Perceptive Crack

Comparison is a crack of immaturity and spiritual imbalance. It reveals a neglect of the Word of God within you, showing that you have prioritized the "*horizontal*" view (others) over the "*vertical*" view (God). To compare is to tell God that His unique design for you was a mistake.

This becomes a foothold when you measure your "*worth*" against another's "*highlight reel.*" This pattern opens the door to **jealousy** ("I want what you have") and **envy** ("I want to be who you are"). You are no longer running your race; you are tripping over someone else's.

This can harden into a **Spirit of Hatred or Bitter Rivalry**. You can no longer celebrate the blessings of others because their success feels like your failure. You become trapped in a cycle of perpetual discontentment.

3. Selfish Desire: The Willful Crack

Selfish desire is the buildup of the "*old man*" that you refused to let die. It reflects a bankrupt prayer life and a lack of authentic communication with God. It is the elevation of *Self* to the throne where the *Spirit* should sit.

This becomes a foothold when you consistently prioritize self-gratification over spiritual discipline. Every time you choose your will over God's, you provide the enemy with the "*legal material*" needed to build a wall around your heart.

This culminates in **Pride,** the ultimate fortification. Pride says, "*I deserve this,*" or "I know better than God." Pride is the high thing that exalts itself against the knowledge of Christ (2 Corinthians 10:4-5). It is the final seal that locks a person into an antichrist mindset, where truth can no longer penetrate.

When you do not address the cracks in your life and neglect your foundation. The result is you destroy your destiny, your calling, and the people around you. The relationship between David and Saul is a perfect example of how insecurity (Saul's crack) led to the destruction of his destiny and his relationships.

I also want to prove to you that if you do not deal with these things, you become part of a body that hosts an Antichrist spirit. This spirit is manifested through specific behaviors we see in Scripture. I once had a vision regarding this manifestation. It is important to understand that when we call on the "Spirit of Elijah," for example, we are not calling on the dead. We are identifying a specific manifestation of the Spirit of God that operated through a man named Elijah. His life and story were an epistle of the Spirit of Might. He restored the altar of the Lord. We have essentially given a name to a specific manifestation of God's Spirit on Earth.

The same principle applies to Jezebel. The "spirit of Jezebel" is not actually the person Jezebel. Instead, it is a manifestation of the Antichrist spirit operating through the human vessel of Jezebel. When we identify the fruit of that manifestation, we can identify the specific spiritual force associated with that human name.

From this revelation, I developed the concept of the Seven Spirits of the Antichrist, which are in perfect opposition to the seven Spirits that conceived and empowered Jesus (Isaiah 11:2). For each Spirit that empowered Jesus, there is a perfect counterfeit. Sometimes manifests into a human personality in scripture.

Antichrist Spirit (Manifestation of the Flesh)	Counterfeit of	The Seven Spirits of God (Isaiah 11:2)
The Snake (Deception)	Opposite of	**Spirit of Truth / The Lord**
Cain (Jealousy/ Murder)	Opposite of	**Spirit of Understanding**
Saul (Insecurity/ Rebellion)	Opposite of	**Spirit of Counsel**
Jezebel (Control/ Manipulation)	Opposite of	**Spirit of Might/ Strength**
Herod (Pride/ Slaughter)	Opposite of	**Spirit of Knowledge**
Religious Leaders (Hypocrisy)	Opposite of	**Spirit of Wisdom**
False Prophets (Lies)	Opposite of	**Spirit of the Fear of the Lord**

I am not going to go deep into this entire concept because I believe it will be in another book. What I am trying to demonstrate, though, is how the crack in these personalities made them eligible to become an instrument—a dead stone—to carry out Satan's objectives.

Let us look at Saul in depth. In the Bible, there are clear moments when Saul manifests the crack of insecurity through behavior that the reader can visibly see. This is evident when David and Saul returned from war, and the women sang songs praising

David a little more than Saul. But even before that moment, we see his deep-seated insecurity and fear. He was afraid to confront the Philistine champion, Goliath. The *crack* was visible for forty days before David stepped onto the field. 1 Samuel 17:11 demonstrates this when it says, *"On hearing the Philistine's words, Saul and all the Israelites were dismayed and greatly afraid."*

From his not fighting Goliath, we see insecurity. From the way he reacted to the song, we see comparison and jealousy. From the way he treated David, we can see the murderous intent and sabotage. David was almost like Saul's spiritual son, yet Saul pursued him relentlessly because of the foothold of insecurity and envy. 1 Samuel 18:7–9 says, *"As they danced, they sang: 'Saul has slain his thousands, and David his tens of thousands.' Saul was very angry... 'What more can he get but the kingdom?' And from that time on, Saul kept a jealous eye on David."*

Furthermore, Saul's unaddressed insecurity led to outright disobedience to God's direct commands, resulting in the loss of his anointing and kingship. This proves a vital point: if it can happen to a person anointed by God, it can happen to you. Saul's downfall is spelled out in the book of 1 Samuel. "But Samuel replied: *'Does the Lord delight in burnt offerings and sacrifices as much as in obeying the Lord? To obey is better than sacrifice... For rebellion is like the sin of divination, and arrogance like the evil of idolatry. Because you have rejected the word of the Lord, he has rejected you as king"* (1 Samuel 15:22-23). Saul's life is a stark warning that a neglected foundation, even in an anointed leader, creates the perfect environment for the enemy to gain a foothold. This ultimately destroys a divine destiny and turns a potential blessing into a bitter curse.

Healing the Cracks: Fortifying the Foundation

The antidote to healing the cracks is found in James 4:7, which says, *"So submit to the authority of God. Resist the devil [stand firm against him], and he will flee from you."* If you cannot resist the devil when temptations arise, you do not have enough Jesus inside of you. Resistance is not just about willpower; it is about filling the cracks with the solid foundation of Christ. This leads your willpower to make the right move, even if it costs your flesh everything. That cost in your flesh is like the feeling of soreness after a good workout. Athletes never run from the feeling. Every time your flesh is denied a selfish desire, and you choose obedience, your spirit is built up and strengthened.

This chapter is not meant to be a moment of accusation or condemnation. That feeling you might feel is simply the light being switched on. Before you clean a dark room, you need to turn on the light so you can see the dirt. Turning on the light, acknowledging the dirt, and making a plan to clean it is the process of deliverance and restoration.

Deliverance and restoration, combined with discipline (repeating the process until we see results), are how we apply the victory of Jesus. That is how we heal the cracks. We keep the light on, trust the truth, and reject the lie day by day. We let love restore us. **"We live in victory every day"**. All of this happens during the 3 crucial stages of illumination I call **salvation, adoption, and discipleship.** These stages are extremely important in the life of a new believer because they **break cycles, restore cracks, and reveal identity**.

It deeply bothers me when churches imply that completing their 'growth track program' (a process for signing up to volunteer in the church building) fulfills the spiritual requirements of **salvation, adoption, or genuine discipleship.** Don't get me wrong, we need community, but you know specifically what I am referring to. The church promises to build up the believer through propaganda, but in reality, they are slowly leading people into exploitation. In certain systems, these "synagogues of Satan" are too busy finding and establishing aesthetic, crafty ways to build slaves for their cause (a parallel world) that they are blinded to the fact that they have become tools Satan uses. They are **violating the souls of inexperienced believers** who come to learn about Jesus. They are robbing those people of God's given mercy, which is time. I grieve this every day. I pray that this book can be a textbook to restore this major crack in the capital "C" Church.

To begin the healing process and solidify your foundation, you must take these practical steps:

Recognize the cracks and behaviors in your life for what they truly are: potential satanic footholds.

Repent, turn on the light, and let go of your self-made identity and desires.

Go back to the stage of illumination you neglected to build completely and correctly; it can be receiving **adoption, receiving salvation, or building discipline** through true discipleship.

The objective of the enemy is to steal, kill, and destroy. He uses limited weapons, disguising their lack of creativity through diverse tactics designed to exploit the cracks you allow in your foundation. He seeks to use your lifeblood, divine potential, and identity in Christ to build the walls of his kingdom. But you have been given the victory through Jesus Christ. By identifying and sealing these cracks, you cut off the enemy's access, dismantle his strongholds, and stop being a "dead stone" used for his purpose. You become a living stone—a dwelling place—where the gates of hell cannot prevail. You become fully equipped to live out your destiny in Christ, which is a goal of Spiritual Warfare.

Chapter 4 — Demon Groupings (Influence, Rank, Territory, And Names)

Now that we've seen how these weapons function, we can go one layer deeper and connect those weapons to the agents of the kingdom of darkness. There are multiple diagrams and frameworks that attempt to explain demonic structure, and some of them can be confusing. I don't believe all of them are wrong. Rather, I believe different people carry different portions of revelation. If those revelations come from the Light, they will overlap in truth, because we only see in part (1 Corinthians 13:12). If those revelations come from corrupted wisdom, they become lies and false narratives—crafted to give glory to a demonic entity so that you can be seduced and subdued.

In the last chapter, we saw how three layers of tactics could regroup a long list of weapons. We uncovered that they were not as inventive as we once believed, after we perceived and acknowledged their final goal. That same clarity applies here. The agents of darkness are those who fell with Satan—lower-ranking members of the angelic order—who operate with a defined end goal.

Demons are builders, and they require territory to establish their works. However, territory cannot be seized without first subduing the owner of that land by exploiting the cracks. A human being is, in fact, territory. To take over a person is to occupy land, both spiritually and physically, because you are a spiritual being residing in human flesh. This is why groupings matter; when you can identify how demons build, where they build, and what kind of territory they seek, you stop reacting in confusion and begin responding with precision.

"How do we group them?" Demons are a coordinated force. Here are the four primary frameworks people use to describe demonic activity.

Primary Frameworks Overview

1. LEVELS OF INFLUENCE — HOW DARKNESS INCREASES ITS INFLUENCE OVER A PERSON.

This framework describes the process:
Temptation → Oppression → Obsession → Suppression → Attachment → Infestation → Possession → Domination

2. RANKINGS OF DEMONS — THE HIERARCHY WITHIN THE KINGDOM OF DARKNESS.

This framework describes *authority and function*:
Principalities, Powers, Rulers of Darkness, Spiritual Wickedness in High Places.

3. THE BIBLICAL MAP OF TERRITORY — REALMS AND DIMENSIONS REFERENCED IN SCRIPTURE.

This framework describes *where* spirits are restrained, operate from, or are destined for:
Sheol/Hades, the Abyss (Bottomless Pit), Tartarus, Gehenna (Lake of Fire), Outer Darkness, and the Grave/Death.

4. TRADITIONAL NAMES OF DEMONS — IDENTIFIERS USED IN SCRIPTURE AND TRADITION.
Apollyon/Abaddon, Belial, Asmodeus, Leviathan, Jezebel, Legion, Python, and others.

These are observations of the same enemy from different angles. We will examine them through four distinct lenses—influence, rank, territory, and names—so that we can speak clearly about what demons do, how they influence, where they operate, who outranks whom, and what a name represents.

Primary Frameworks Explained

1. LEVELS OF INFLUENCE — HOW DARKNESS INCREASES ITS INFLUENCE OVER A PERSON.

Darkness increases its influence over a person through the strategic process of temptation. As we covered in Chapter 2, this is a systematic method of 'possession,' a step-by-step spectrum that moves from a mere suggestion to total domination. The enemy's objective is to steal, kill, and destroy by turning a "living stone" into a "dead stone," a vessel fully occupied by demonic forces. We must expose these levels so that our resistance can be made whole.

Temptation is the initial stage where a few spirits test the "cracks" in your foundation. This comes as a suggestion or proposal —like the 'fiery arrows by day.' These are intrusive thoughts or sudden urges that a healthy conscience quickly dismisses. However, when you accept the proposal, you grant them permission to enter. Once inside, they creatively inspire you with invitations to act on that proposal and sin.

This escalates to **oppression,** where demons apply external pressure and binding. This manifests as chronic anxiety, heaviness, or unexplained physical distress. At this stage, the enemy is working to apply enough pressure to create even more cracks to exploit.

If unaddressed, this leads to obsession. **Obsession** reveals a *"legion"* strategy, where the mind is dominated by intrusive, repetitive, sinful thoughts and fixations. The goal is to bombard you until your will is bound. As you remain passive, they bring in more spirits to prepare for the next stage.

Here, the 'Captains'—higher-ranking coordinating spirits—take their place. Your spirit man is now tied down; you may know the truth, but you can barely stop the system that has been built in your mind. Human emotions are **suppressed** while demonic emotions rise, building thick walls in the soul.

Attachment occurs when a spirit successfully claims a specific area of life, such as anger or fear. The result is a habitual sin pattern that slowly alters your spiritual "DNA," making it difficult to break cycles.

This allows for **infestation**, where patterns of destruction manifest in your physical environment, health, or finances. They leave a mark on your lineage so the fortress can be built in your children and your children's children.

Possession is the culmination of the enemy's agenda—the full or partial occupation of the body and mind. The territory is now conquered. The host's body becomes a *"dead stone,"* a house full of legions where spirits have seized control of the faculties.

In this final and most severe stage, the individual's will and identity are nearly erased and replaced by a demonic identity. The person becomes a host—**dominated**—for Satan's objectives on earth, an instrument used for his purposes—whether dead or alive.

A Warning About Empty Houses

In Matthew 12:43–45, when an impure spirit is cast out and finds its former house "unoccupied, swept clean, and put in order," it returns with seven other spirits more wicked than itself. This reveals the *"family"* or *"team"* strategy of demons. Deliverance is a gift, but it must be led by the Spirit. Delivering a person outside of the Spirit's guidance, without filling the house with the Presence of God, exposes them to a more wicked re-occupation. Demons return as a team to re-secure their territory.

To kill these levels of possession, you must have the capacity to offer spiritual sacrifices. Fasting and prayer are sacrifices that provide the authority to cast out dominion and kill the seeds of dominion within yourself. Jesus told His disciples they were "small in faith" because they lacked this discipline. I believe a disciple of Jesus should practice spiritual disciplines like fasting and prayer. This is not just a ritual; it is a necessity to remain sober, clean, and to cleanse your spiritual life. By doing so, you ensure your "house" is never unoccupied, but is instead filled with the Light that no darkness can overcome.

2. RANKINGS OF DEMONS — THE HIERARCHY WITHIN THE KINGDOM OF DARKNESS.

This hierarchy was already introduced and established in Section V, Chapter 2, through the Apostle Paul's framework in Ephesians 6:12. We revisit it here not to repeat doctrine, but to apply it within the context of Demons Grouping.

The hierarchy includes Principalities, Powers, Rulers of Darkness, and Spiritual Wickedness in High Places.

Paul defines these ranks clearly:
"For our struggle is not against flesh and blood, but against the rulers [Principalities], against the authorities [Powers], against the cosmic powers of this darkness [Rulers of Darkness of This World], against the spiritual forces of wickedness in the heavenly realms." (Ephesians 6:12)

3. THE BIBLICAL MAP OF TERRITORY — REALMS AND DIMENSIONS REFERENCED IN SCRIPTURE.

Scripture reveals that the realm of darkness has boundaries, prisons, and an end. This map exposes the system demons are building toward and the urgency of stopping their work while time remains.

The dimensions mentioned in Scripture—Sheol/Hades, the Abyss, Tartarus, Gehenna, Outer Darkness, and the Grave—reveal this structure.

The Bible also speaks of the "gates of hell." When Jesus said that these gates would not prevail, He was revealing that this dark territory is attempting to press into our realm of time.

This matters because it reveals the complete absence of God's presence in these realms. Many cultures mistakenly view the afterlife as a waiting place for rewards, but this view is flawed. An afterlife without God is, by definition, hell. Since all true life comes from God, the final rejection of Him—the Source of Life—leads to decay and separation. Hell stands as the contrast that reveals the value of God's presence.

The Grave / Death — The Physical End
Hebrew: קֶבֶר (*Qeber*, specific grave)
Greek: θάνατος (*Thanatos*, death)
Meaning: *Qeber* refers to a physical burial place, while *Thanatos* refers to physical death—the separation of the body and the spirit. This is the visible end of biological life, not yet the final judgment.

Sheol / Hades — The Temporary Abode
Hebrew: שְׁאוֹל (*She'ol*)
Greek: Ἅδης (*Hadēs*)

Meaning: Sheol is described in the Old Testament as a shadowy, silent place in the depths of the earth where souls went after death. It represents a temporary state of separation from the living, distinct from eternal punishment.

In the New Testament, Hades is sometimes depicted as having separation within it—between the righteous (often referred to as Abraham's Bosom) and the wicked (a place of torment), divided by a great and unbridgeable gulf. This separation ensures that those at rest are permanently divided from those in torment.

Temporary Prisons / The Holding Cells

These are specialized *"custody"* realms where spiritual beings are restrained until the final sentence is passed.

The Abyss (Bottomless Pit)
Greek: ἄβυσσος *(Abyssos)*

Meaning: A deep place of confinement for specific demons and spirits. It is a place of temporary restraint, where Satan himself will be bound during the Millennium (Revelation 20:1–3).

Tartarus
Greek: ταρταρόω *(tartaróō)*

Meaning: Mentioned in 2 Peter 2:4, Tartarus is the deepest prison. It is reserved for specific fallen angels who broke rank, holding them in "chains of darkness" until the Day of Judgment.

Outer Darkness
Greek: τὸ σκότος τὸ ἐξώτερον *(to skotos to exōteron)*

Meaning: A state of extreme separation from God's light, described by Jesus as a place of profound regret and sorrow— "weeping and gnashing of teeth."

Final Judgment: The Permanent Destination

Gehenna / Lake of Fire
Hebrew: גֵּיא בֶן־הִנֹּם *(Gei Ben Hinnom, Valley of Hinnom)*
Greek: γέεννα *(Geenna)*

Meaning: A literal valley outside ancient Jerusalem, historically associated with burning refuse and bodies. Jesus used this imagery to describe the final place of eternal judgment. In Revelation, this is revealed as the Lake of Fire—the permanent destination where both body and soul are destroyed (Matthew 10:28).

4. TRADITIONAL NAMES OF DEMONS — IDENTIFIERS USED IN SCRIPTURE AND TRADITION

Psychology does not replace deliverance. It does give us a language to understand how groups of demons organize themselves through traits, behaviors, and patterns. Psychology can describe the pattern, but only the Holy Spirit can break the legal ground beneath it.

In this section, we establish a simple but powerful principle: **traits are spirits, and personality is the stronghold that hosts them.** This framework is for discernment, not diagnosis. Psychology becomes a natural framework that displays the mechanisms of the human operating system. The Holy Spirit provides the manual, and the solution will always be Jesus' light.

These are names of demons such as Apollyon/Abaddon, Belial ("worthlessness"), Asmodeus, Leviathan, Jezebel, Legion, and Python (a spirit of divination). These names highlight a specific, identifiable nature or "personality trait" of that spirit's influence. Spiritually, these names tell us what type of personality a spirit will build inside a person.

When these evil spirits regroup inside a person's life, they are working to build a structure on earth. A possessed or heavily influenced individual becomes that physical manifestation of the "building" where these spirits reside and operate. The human body serves as the vessel—the "dead stone" host—that gives a spiritual entity access to operate within the physical realm. They are forming an army on earth, operating through human vessels to carry out the objectives of darkness until their final judgment in the Lake of Fire.

1. A Spirit is a Personality: Traits and Fruits

In psychology, a personality trait is a stable pattern of behavior, thought, or emotion that builds a unique personality. Psychology provides names for these patterns, but spiritually, we know the deeper reality behind them. Traits are spirits; personality is the strongman through which they express themselves. Our core assertion is that traits are external expressions of internal spiritual realities. The consistent, stable personality we observe is the stronghold, or the "strong man" (Matthew 12:29), empowered by a group of cooperating spirits.

Psychology uses models like the Big Five personality traits (Openness, Conscientiousness, Extraversion, Agreeableness, and Neuroticism) to map human personality. These dimensions display consistent clusters of traits that mirror the grouping of spirits. For example, Neuroticism manifests as anxiety, fear, worry, moodiness, and sadness that cluster predictably. Spiritually, this cluster might be identified as *"spirits of fear"* or *"spirits of depression."* Low agreeableness involves traits such as manipulation, hostility, apathy, and selfishness—all hallmarks of the "Jezebel" or "Belial" types of influence.

When a deliverance minister observes these consistent clusters of traits, they are not just identifying a psychological pattern. They are identifying the signature of a specific type of spirit or group of spirits. The persistence and severity of these traits beyond normal human variation suggest a non-human origin. Just like the Holy Spirit manifests a clear set of fruits: *love, joy, peace, kindness, and self-control* (Galatians 5:22-23).

2. Behavior as a Reflection of Spirituality

Your behavior often reflects your underlying spiritual state. Just like we can recognize someone's personality based on their actions, we can discern their spiritual alignment by the fruits or traits they exhibit. This behavioral manifestation is a way to identify spiritual progress or regression. Someone who shows kindness and patience is likely under the influence of the Holy Spirit, while someone who shows anger, selfishness, and envy might be influenced by negative spirits or desires. Psychology calls these patterns "behavioral expressions," but spiritually we call them the fruits of the Spirit or the fruits of darkness.

3. Sin and Conceiving Behavior: The "Crack" and the Stronghold

The biblical process of sin makes perfect sense within a psychological framework that explains how a personality trait moves from an internal inclination to an external action. The crack can also be the result of trauma at the entry point. Ephesians 4:27 says, *"Give no place to the devil."* Psychology helps us identify exactly where that "place" is.

Cognitive Behavioral Theory (CBT) holds that our thoughts (desires/temptations) drive our feelings and behaviors (sins/actions). When a spirit injects a thought (e.g., "You are worthless") and the person dwells on it (conception), it becomes a core belief and manifests in behavior (e.g., self-sabotage, addiction, or sin). This progression explains how an initial "crack" of sin becomes a deeply entrenched personality stronghold.

The Behavioral Loop explains this process. Sin starts as an internal desire or temptation, much as a personality trait begins as an inclination before it manifests in action. James 1:14-15 shows how sin is conceived through desire and grows into behavior.

That behavior, if left unchecked, leads to death. *"But each one is tempted when he is dragged away, enticed and baited to commit sin by his own worldly desire (lust, passion). Then when the desire has conceived, it gives birth to sin; and when sin has run its course, it gives birth to death"* (James 1:14-15). This loop reinforces new neural pathways. The spirit is literally changing the host's brain chemistry and physically embodying that sin. Psychology describes it as neuroplasticity. Spiritually, it is the process by which the host is shaped into the image of the spirit influencing them.

4. The Embodiment of Darkness

The psychology of Identity Formation and Role Theory supports the vision of spirits "building a body" through a human vessel. The concept of internal "parts" or identities provides a useful analogy for how a person might give internal "room" for a spirit to operate. This leads to the embodiment of traits. When a person constantly acts out of anger, that anger becomes "embodied." It changes their physical posture, their facial expressions, and even their neural pathways. The spirit gains a tangible presence by literally changing the host's physical brain and body chemistry. The *"dead stone"* becomes a functional structure for the "spiritual entity." Psychology would say the person is "internalizing a trait." Spiritually, we know they are housing a spirit.

Based on the trait and the behavior of the personal manifestation, we can identify the group of demons, the stronghold, and the precise "crack" through which they entered. We can also uncover why they stay. Psychology offers a brilliant framework and display of discernment that can help deliverance ministers, if it is explained and applied correctly. It is a powerful, yet incomplete, science without deliverance. Psychology displays the mechanisms of the human operating system. The Holy Spirit provides the manual; the solution will always be Jesus' light.

The Map of Demon Groupings

A unified biblical–psychological classification
Demons organize themselves into clusters, families, and functional groupings. These clusters reflect consistent psychological patterns, biblical descriptions, and spiritual assignments. Below is the unified map.

1. Bitterness Group

Included Spirits: Resentment, hatred, unforgiveness, murder.

Root Function: Bitterness keeps replaying past trauma. It is often directed toward family or early relationships.

Psychology Link: Rumination loops, trauma fixation, emotional reactivity.

Entry Points: Offense, injustice, betrayal, unresolved conflict.

4. Rejection Group

2. Rebellion Group

Included Spirits: Stubbornness, disobedience, anti-submissiveness, antichrist spirit.

Root Function: Rebellion is the spirit of antichrist. It refuses to honor divine or human authority.

Psychology Link: Oppositional behavior, defiance cycles, authority trauma.

Entry Points: Pride, father wounds, anti-authority environments.

5. Depression Group

Included Spirits: Despair, hopelessness, suicide,

3. Control Group

Included Spirits: Witchcraft, dominance, manipulation, possessiveness.

Root Function: Control masquerades as protection. It appears in marriages, parenting, friendships, and even pastoral leadership.

Psychology Link: Overcompensation, fear-driven control, trauma-informed dominance.

Entry Points: Fear, insecurity, loss of power, chaotic childhoods.

6. Fear & Anxiety Group

Included Spirits: Worry, dread, fear of

Included Spirits: Rejection, Fear of rejection, self-rejection.

Root Function: Rejection often begins in the womb. It operates as a three-headed spirit: Rejection, fear of rejection, and self-rejection.

Psychology Link: Attachment trauma, negative self-concept, abandonment internalization.

Entry Points: Womb trauma, parental neglect, early emotional wounds

7. Mental Illness / Mind-Binding Group
Included Spirits:

insomnia.

Root Function: Depression locks a person in emotional darkness and robs them of hope.

Psychology Link: Mood dysregulation, learned helplessness, trauma loops.

Entry Points: Prolonged pain, grief, spiritual bondage

8. Sexual Impurity Group
Included Spirits: All Lust, masturbation, pornography, adultery, incest, frigidity & sexual binding.

Root Function: These spirits target appetite,

man, panic attacks, phobias, idolatry.

Root Function: Fear torments. Anxiety destabilizes thinking and magnifies danger.

Psychology Link: Catastrophic thinking, hypervigilance, anxiety disorders.

Entry Points: Childhood trauma, instability, sudden crisis.

9. Addiction Group
Included Spirits: Alcohol, nicotine, medication dependence, compulsive habits.

Root Function: Addiction is a false refuge and a counterfeit comfort.

Psychology Link: Escape behavior, dependency cycles,

Confusion, mind-binding, schizophrenia, paranoia, pharmakia.

Root Function: These spirits attack cognition, clarity, and soundness of mind.

Psychology Link: Identity fracturing, intrusive thoughts, trauma-induced dissociation.

Entry Points: Abuse, drug abuse, generational bondage, occult exposure.

10. Religious Error Group

pleasure, and connection.

Psychology Link: Reward-system hijacking, compulsive behaviors, trauma eroticization.

Entry Points: Sexual abuse, media exposure, generational sin.

11. Pride & Vanity Group
Included Spirits: Pride, arrogance, superiority, comparison, perfectionism, self-exaltation, self-righteousness.

Root Function: False identity, performance, distorted perception of one self.

emotional avoidance.

Entry Points: Pain, stress, trauma, coping breakdown.

12. Trauma & Fragmentation Group
Included Spirits: Brokenness, dissociation, fear-driven identity splits, inner fragmentation.

Root Function: Overwhelming trauma, Generational traumas, lack of light because of generational traumas, root of many identity issues, perfect ground for demons to break in.

Included Spirits: Legalism, doctrinal deception, false humility, occult influence, God complex.

Root Function: Religious spirits bind believers with counterfeit "truth", fear, and confusion.

Psychology Link: Cognitive rigidity, moral absolutism, authority dependence, lack of empathy.

Entry Points: False teaching, pride, lack of discipleship, spiritual abuse.

Psychology Link: Narcissistic defenses Grandiosity Image-based identity Shame-driven perfectionism

Entry Points: Insecurity, Achievement-based childhood, Rejection (overcompensated through superiority), Trauma masked by self-exaltation.

Psychology Link: Dissociation Fragmented identity, Hyperarousal, PTSD symptoms, Emotional flashbacks

Entry Points: Sexual abuse, generational sexual sin, occult binding, Chronic trauma, Early childhood neglect, Repeated emotional injury, Violent or shocking experiences.

Up to now, we have covered many topics. We uncovered the system, the patterns, the entry points, and the way darkness tries to build a parallel world inside a human vessel. We will now shift our attention to the effective weapons against the enemy. Now that you can recognize the system, we can finally move to the solution that collapses it: Light. Spiritual warfare is like the work of an entomologist who studies insects. You study darkness and demons the same way an entomologist studies roaches. It is not because I know what the roach can do that I give the roach power over me—it is because I know what it is, and I know how to remove it.

Section VI

The Effective Weapons Against The Devil

Chapter 1 — Knowing God — His Position, His Truth, And His Love

GOD'S POSITION — WHO GOD IS IN RELATION TO ALL THINGS

Before we can use any weapon in spiritual warfare, we need to recognize that God is the one who designed, empowers, and makes these weapons effective. Standing against the enemy depends first on you grasping God's unique position, His unmatched authority, and your identity in relation to Him. This knowledge is the primary weapon in spiritual warfare.

Our identity is intrinsically linked to the One who created you. How can one being create a human race so diverse and intricate? We only have a partial idea of who God is, and that perception will only be complete in the afterlife. The Bible says in Revelation that all creatures and saints continuously rediscover a new facet of Him.

They are so enthralled by His majesty that their only response is awe and worship.

I believe it takes a lifetime just to know even a small portion of God. While some people might find this intimidating, I find it exciting. God reveals Himself to us through seasons. We gain new awareness of His character as we grow and mature.

Before moving forward, however, it is crucial to transition from knowing God's character to recognizing His supreme position in relation to the universe. This is a foundational step in any effective approach to spiritual warfare.

Recognizing His authority enables full trust in His victory and unmasks the adversary's central lies. Everything else depends on this recognition.

Here is a practical example: would you trust me more for directions if I were on a bicycle or if I were in an airplane? If I'm in an airplane, my vision is vast enough to give you expansive, reliable instructions. If I'm on a bicycle, my vision is limited. My directions wouldn't be suitable for long-term guidance.

Likewise, God's position offers a cosmic, limitless view of your life and every included spiritual realm.

Many misunderstandings about God's position have developed over centuries and cultures. An example of a common incorrect belief is that God and the adversary are equals locked in battle. In reality, God is immeasurably greater. The evil one is not on His level and is not His equal in any way.

As we explore the effective weapons against darkness, keep this central truth in view. Grasping God's supreme position is essential. Actively seek clarity on why He is who He says He is. This foundation empowers every stage of spiritual warfare.

We hear many attributes of God in the Bible and in church, but do we truly perceive them? Honestly, I don't think we fully do—because we are not moved by them. Here is a list of some of His attributes. Let us picture them from a cosmic view:

Omnipresent — God Is Everywhere

Because God exists beyond the limits of the cosmos, He fills all of creation at once. There is no location where His presence is absent.

"Do I not fill the heavens and the earth?" (Jeremiah 23:24)

Omnipotent — God Is All-Powerful

God's power is not restricted by matter, time, dimension, or any created force. Every form of energy in the universe answers to Him.

"The Lord God the Almighty reigns." (Revelation 19:6)

Righteous — God Is Morally Perfect

Within the vast moral order of the universe, God is the unchanging standard of purity. His character is flawless and incapable of corruption.

"For the Lord is righteous; He loves righteous deeds." (Psalm 11:7)

Patient — God's Patience Is Eternal

God is so patient that He created time and space themselves as a mercy, giving humanity room to repent, return, and be restored. His patience is a deliberate stretching of eternity so, we are given the opportunity to choose Him.

"The Lord does not delay… but is extraordinarily patient toward you…" (2 Peter 3:9)

Without grasping God's position, attributes such as omnipresence and omnipotence can feel abstract and difficult to visualize. For this reason, recognizing God's position is essential for anchoring faith and giving these attributes meaning.

Now that we have examined why knowing God's position is vital, we can transition to defining the actual stage on which spiritual reality unfolds: the cosmos.

The word *cosmos* comes from the Greek word κόσμος *(kosmos)*, meaning *order* or *world*. Over time, it expanded to mean *the universe* or *a harmonious, ordered system*. Ancient Greek philosophers used this term to describe universal order and beauty in contrast to chaos. It later entered Latin and English with the same sense of unity and structure.

The universe is the totality of all space, time, matter, and energy. It includes all galaxies, stars, planets, and celestial bodies. These are governed by physical laws and constants.

Physical laws are universal principles that regulate how the universe behaves, ensuring consistency and predictability. Physical constants are specific, unchanging values—such as the speed of light or the strength of gravity—that shape fundamental forces.

Together, these laws and constants maintain order, structure, and fine-tuning, allowing galaxies, stars, planets, and life itself to exist.

The universe includes both what we can see—such as the sun and the moon—and what we cannot see, such as invisible forces. Everything operates according to established rules. These rules include physical laws and spiritual laws, which explain how reality functions both naturally and spiritually.

The Universe's Beginning and Contingency

When we study the universe, one of the first things we discover is that the cosmos had a beginning. This is not merely a theological belief; it is a scientific conclusion. Through astronomy, cosmology, and physics, we see clear evidence that the universe is not eternal. It expands, it ages, and it traces back to a single starting point. This means the universe is not self-existent. It came into being at a specific moment.

The second discovery is that the universe cannot sustain itself. Everything within it—from stars burning out to galaxies drifting apart—reveals dependency. Scientific laws show that nothing in the cosmos has the power to create itself or uphold itself indefinitely. This means the universe is what philosophers call **contingent**: it relies on something outside of itself to exist, function, and continue.

From these observations, scientists and philosophers agree that the universe must have an external cause—something or someone greater who initiated it and sustains it. Scripture identifies this cause in Genesis 1:1: *"In the beginning God (Elohim) created the heavens and the earth."* Here, the scientific picture aligns with biblical revelation: the universe depends on God. John 1 takes us even deeper into the spiritual reality behind the physical world: *"In the beginning [before all time] was the Word (Christ)... All things were made and came into existence through Him"* (John 1:1–3). Together, science and Scripture point to the same truth: the universe exists because God willed it, shaped it, and continues to sustain it— moment by moment—through the tangible expression of Himself: Christ.

The Universe's Scope and Cosmology

When we look at the universe through the study of cosmology— the science of the origin and development of the universe—we begin to see something powerful. Creation is precise. It is intentional, ordered, and alive with profound meaning.

Everything in the cosmos, from the smallest subatomic particle flickering in the unseen quantum realm to massive galaxies stretching across billions of light-years, is held together by laws so exact they cannot be accidental. These physical laws—gravity, electromagnetism, and nuclear forces—function like the invisible hand of a Designer.

The universe is not static. It is continually expanding, moving outward from a singular point of origin that science calls the Big Bang. Cosmology attempts to explain the structure, origins, and laws that govern the universe, yet in doing so, it ultimately traces the outline of God's craftsmanship.

Every physical constant, every force, every mathematical precision silently declares a singular truth: Someone built this.

This is why Scripture speaks with such authority. Psalm 19:1 declares:

"The heavens are telling of the glory of God; and the expanse [of heaven] is declaring the work of His hands."

Creation does not whisper; creation testifies. The heavens preach without a pulpit. The galaxies worship without a song. Everything in the cosmos points back to one Designer, one supreme Intelligence, one Source.

God created the cosmos. That means He stands outside of time, above creation, ruling from a position no being can challenge. Jesus is seated with Him in the heavenly places, far above every realm, dimension, and spiritual power. If God exists beyond the boundaries of time and space, then Jesus also operates from that same eternal position.

When you grasp God's position, trust becomes natural. When you acknowledge that He created all things, it becomes instinctive to turn to Him for everything. You trust His direction because He sees from eternity. You trust His truth because He *is* truth. You trust His instruction because nothing in existence is hidden from His view.

Bringing this cosmic perspective back to a personal level, I see the universe as a vast and beautiful canvas—an intricate stage carefully established by God and sustained through Jesus Christ for humanity. The universe constantly reflects God's greatness and supreme authority. Let this draw you toward the purposeful Creator, and recognize that acknowledging His authority is one of your greatest weapons in spiritual warfare.

This is why Satan does everything in his power to sever that connection between you and God. The enemy knows that the moment God's true position is recognized, trust becomes unshakeable. And once trust is established, your foundation becomes immovable.

You no longer lean on fear, confusion, or the limitations of your own perspective. You lean on the One who stands above all things, outside all things, and sustains all things.

Knowing God's position is the first victory in spiritual warfare.

GOD'S TRUTH — WHAT BELONGS TO GOD ALONE

We live in a generation where truth has become *"fluid,"* subjective, and completely shaped by emotion. Culture now tells you that you can create your *own* truth, which implies that morality is purely personal. But if morality and truth are personal, if we can reshape them whenever we feel like it, then there is no absolute truth. There is no universal morality. There is only a list of personal preferences dressed up as genuine conviction.

Scripture, however, teaches the opposite. If we did not create the heavens and the earth, nor did we design the universe, its order, its physical laws, or the invisible forces that govern it, then we certainly did not create the truth. Truth is one of the pillars of God's order. It is unchanging, established, and eternal. Truth is not something humans invent. It is something we discover and then choose to submit to.

This generation is experiencing exactly what the Bible warned us about:

"And all will turn their ears away from the truth and will wander off into myths and man-made fictions [and will accept the unacceptable]" (2 Timothy 4:4).

There is no need to be surprised or to panic. Our focus is not on reacting to cultural shifts; our focus is on being refined by eternal principles. Without this pillar of absolute truth, your foundation in spiritual warfare will always be shaky. The enemy depends on your lack of truth to deceive you. He relies on confusion, instability, and emotional reasoning to gain access to your life. After reading this book, you will not only understand the truth, but you will also become a lover of the truth. You will love the truth even when that truth goes against your personal preferences.

Truth belongs to God, not us

What Is The Truth? Truth is more than just a fact. Truth is a force that leads anything into a specific order, from foundation to expression. The force of Truth originates from the core part of the personality of God, present in all His manifestations and everything He has created.

In Scripture, the very word *truth* carries a depth worth examining. In Hebrew, *"emet"* means "firmness, stability, something that stands unshakable." It refers to something reliable, established, and permanent. It operates like a force with a distinct personality, a clear direction, and a set order.

In Greek, *aletheia* means what is unveiled, disclosed, or with nothing hidden". It refers to reality as it truly is, stripped of all distortion, illusion, or deception. It reveals what exists from foundation to ultimate expression, opposing all forms of distortion.

This is why one of God's names in Scripture is *El Emet,* the *"God of Truth"* in the Hebrew Bible (e.g., Psalm 31:5). This name implies that truth belongs to Him inherently because it is part of Him. He is the ultimate, faithful, and reliable source of all that is real and stable, including morality itself.

From the beginning of this chapter, we learned foundational truths about God's position in the cosmos:

- God exists outside the cosmos, the universe He created.
- Jesus existed before anything was created or came into being.
- All creation flows from His nature, His will, and His established order.

From this, we can draw a clear and powerful conclusion regarding the origin of all reality: If God created Creation, He created the Truth that governs Creation.

The physical laws—such as gravity or thermodynamics—and the spiritual laws—such as sowing and reaping—are expressions of God's consistent and truthful nature. Truth functions as the operating system of the universe. It cannot be changed, manipulated, or voted away. It can only be discovered and obeyed.

Our success in spiritual warfare depends entirely on operating within the boundaries of God's established truth.

Because truth existed before creation, before humanity, and before time itself, it cannot originate from human emotion, opinion, or experience. Truth transcends subjective reality. It stands because

God stands. It does not change because God does not change. It is firm because God is firm, and it endures because God endures.

This is why truth ultimately belongs to God and not to us.

Your opinions can shift. Your feelings can fluctuate. Your experiences are temporary. Truth is not. It remains the same yesterday, today, and forever. And because truth belongs to God, knowing the truth is what sets you free.

Satan's primary strategy is to distort this reality. He tells people that truth is subjective—that it is equal to preference. He feeds thoughts that sound like this: *"If I prefer this and it makes me feel good, then that feeling must be my truth."*

But if that claim were true, it would have to be applied consistently. For example, if someone believes they have the right to hate an entire group because they were harmed by one individual, then others would have the same right to hate the group that person belongs to for the same reason. If a "truth" cannot be constant and universally applicable, it is not truth at all. It is a preference—used to justify pride.

This mindset mirrors the nature of Satan himself.

The belief that you can create your own truth is the same belief that you can create your own reality. It is the attempt to build a parallel world apart from God. And if you are not aligned with the truth of God, you are inevitably aligned with the desire of Satan, which is the lie.

Why Satan Attacks The Truth

Satan is limited in both power and position. He cannot attack God's ultimate authority or throne. Instead, he attacks the one thing he can reach: **your relationship with the One who embodies Truth**.

Scripture makes this clear.
2 Corinthians 4:4 says that the *"god of this world"* blinds the minds of unbelievers so they cannot see the truth.
Hosea 4:6 declares that people perish for lack of knowledge—not because truth does not exist, but because it is rejected, distorted, or ignored.

If Satan can separate you from physical Truth, Jesus Christ, he can separate you from freedom.

If he can separate you from the template of Truth, Jesus Christ, he can separate you from your identity and destiny.

If he can separate you from the order of Truth, he can prevent you from establishing the victory of Jesus that is already accessible to you.

Truth is not passive.
Truth is a weapon.
Truth is a piece of your armor that stabilizes you in battle.
Truth is also light. And by both physical and spiritual law, darkness cannot overpower light (John 1:5). Spiritual warfare begins with accepting that truth belongs to God. A mature Christian recognizes truth, loves truth, and submits to it.

If you are reading this part of the book, you are not a spiritual infant—you are someone who understands that truth is a foundation a mature believer cultivates with joy.

When truth is alive in you, it produces Christlike behavior. That behavior looks like wisdom, clarity, discernment, critical thinking, moral integrity, awareness, and sound judgment. Without these, the mind becomes spiritually unstable and easily influenced.

This is why a mature believer actively seeks truth in the Word of God, submits to it, and becomes a doer of it. They surrender their opinions to truth in order to receive transformation by light. Scripture says plainly that *"obedience to the truth purifies the soul"* (1 Peter 1:22).

A believer grounded in truth cannot be easily deceived, diluted, or dragged into confusion. Many people try to fight confusion directly, but fighting confusion without first establishing truth is like putting a bandage on a wound that is still bleeding.

The spirit of lying is the first enemy of truth. If one of God's defining attributes is the Spirit of Truth, then Satan's defining nature is the spirit of lying. Opposing truth is his primary strategy and the root of every deception encountered in spiritual warfare.

This spirit never operates alone. It always brings a cluster with it: lying, dishonor, rebellion, fear of man, deceit, exaggeration, gossip, cursing, murmuring, manipulation, speech perversion, and distortion. Together, these spirits work to cloud judgment, break discernment, and reshape reality.

They oppose truth because they oppose Christ Himself—the embodiment of truth. Confusion is the signature of Satan's kingdom. Scripture reminds us clearly that *God is not the author of confusion* (1 Corinthians 14:33). Wherever God's truth stands, clarity follows, and clarity creates a secure position for battle.

After everything we have uncovered, one conclusion becomes unavoidable: **truth is essential for victory**.

If truth existed before creation and belongs to God…
If truth is one of the Seven Spirits of Christ…
If truth defines the Holy Spirit…
If truth is the absence of darkness and the force that holds reality

together…
If truth protects the soul and sets it free…

Then this must also be true:
Truth has divine order.
Truth is a weapon.
Truth is a shield.
Truth fights for you.
Truth exposes darkness.
Truth does not belong to you, but it can live in you.
Truth, in its entirety, belongs to God.

As you prepare to explore the next effective weapon—love—hold fast to this unshakable principle:
Only the truth that comes from God can defeat the lies of Satan.
Only the truth you submit to can set you free.
And only the truth you choose to live in can make you victorious in spiritual warfare.

GOD'S LOVE — THE HIGHEST FORM OF POWER

To be honest, delving into the concept of love in this book—especially the love of God—humbles me deeply. This humility, mixed with conviction, continually draws me back to God. There is no better place than being small, full of reverence, at His feet. That is where I find my true place, and it gives me peace.

As I've explored and studied love as a weapon, I've come to realize something essential: fully comprehending the love that *is* God is beyond human capability. And yet, God still invites us to discover it. Acknowledging that the full scope of God's love cannot be grasped is not a limitation—it is wisdom.

Just as truth is a force, **love is the power of that force**. I do not want to be presumptuous and claim complete understanding. From both a spiritual and intellectual perspective, the love of God is a profound mystery—one that unfolds over a lifetime and continues revealing its depth even beyond the life we live.

So, what exactly is love?

Scripture tells us plainly: **God is love**. If we attempt to name it— to describe what love *is*—I define it as a force that flows from a **Supreme, multidimensional, supernatural entity**.

Why? Because love is not an object we can see or measure. Even if it were visible, it would still feel subjective. And yet, it leaves unmistakably objective marks. Love resonates. Love transforms. Love alters reality.

Here is a clearer expansion of those core components:

Supreme

This implies ultimate sovereignty, indicating that this entity is the highest-ranking and original source of all existence. It possesses absolute power and authority, standing above all other forces or beings. It is the uncreated creator, the origin point from which all dimensions, laws, and realities derive their existence.

Multidimensional

This component means the entity exists and functions across an infinite number of layers of reality simultaneously. This includes spiritual realms, physical universes, emotional planes, mental spheres, and other unseen dimensions. The entity is not confined to our perception of a single space, time continuum, or physical form, but can manifest or engage within any or all of them seamlessly.

Supernatural

This signifies an existence that operates entirely beyond conventional natural laws as understood in the physical universe. This entity is not bound by physical rules such as gravity, linear time, or distance. It possesses innate power, intelligence, and a capacity for function that vastly transcends all human abilities and scientific understanding. Its operations involve phenomena that cannot be explained or contained within the natural order.

Entity

This element confirms a personal aspect. It is a being with a distinct identity, conscious nature, will, and purpose. It is not an impersonal, abstract energy field or a mere philosophical idea, but rather a living, aware being capable of interaction, relationship, and intentional action.

This terminology attempts to name that which transcends human descriptors—a singular being that encompasses infinite existence without being contained by it. That Being is God.

The Anatomy of Love

God's love also has a nature that can be observed and understood. This is similar to how anatomy reveals how a body functions. We uncover this "anatomy" by observing how God expresses His nature throughout Scripture.

God revealed Himself to people, and through the record of their lived encounters with Him. The functionality of divine love became visible to us. Scripture demonstrates how it moves, acts, heals, confronts, restores, and redeems.

We use human language to describe this reality, while remembering that God is not human. These terms are not definitions —they are frameworks that help us grasp a divine truth. This anatomy allows us to see how love, as both a force and a person, operates across all dimensions of reality.

The Anatomy of Love as Revealed in God:

Function
To resurrect, heal, reveal truth, and direct human lives with purpose.

Direction
Starting from God's Spirit, through God's Spirit, to get to God's Spirit in full at the end

Identity
Everything is revealed through the Son of God.

Purpose
To bring humanity back to God, safe, redeemed, and restored

Essence (a force)
The Holy Spirit

Tangible Body
Jesus

Love's Function

To Resurrect — *"I Am the Life"*

Jesus is our primary lens. It is through His physical presence and actions that the invisible function of God's love becomes visible and understandable.

Through the tangible lens of Jesus, the Bible speaks of what I call the *resurrecting power*. This part of the authority of love is visible in multiple dimensions, linking the function of resurrection directly to *"I Am Life."* Because Jesus is full of life, the life in Him is enough to fill the missing life in you, which is resurrection.

John 11:25—*"Jesus said to her, 'I am the resurrection and the life. The one who believes in me will live, even though they die."* Romans 8:11—*"And if the Spirit of him who raised Jesus from the dead is living in you, he who raised Christ from the dead will also give life to your mortal bodies because of his Spirit who lives in you."*

Even in day-to-day life, love exhibits a power of resurrection. From a psychological and observational standpoint, love can metaphorically *"resurrect"* a person's spirit from despair. The profound impact of genuine human connection, mirroring divine love, restores hope and life to those who are broken.

Did you know that your connection with casting out demons is linked to your ability to carry the resurrecting power that Christ Jesus is? Which is part of the anatomy of love.

To Heal to Reveal, and Reveal to Heal – *"I Am the Truth"*

- **To Heal to Reveal**

To understand the combined functions of healing and revealing, we continue to use the Tangible Body (Jesus) as our primary lens. Jesus perfectly embodies the concepts of **light, truth, and love**, which are entirely synonymous in the divine anatomy. His teachings, life, and ultimate sacrifice demonstrate how these concepts are profoundly intertwined. Conversely, **lies, fear, and darkness** are also synonymous—and they stand in direct opposition to love's nature.

Because Jesus is Truth, Love, and Light, His presence illuminates and guides us, immediately transcending any darkness. His manifestation of love led directly to His exaltation, demonstrating that love operates from a position of authority and victory.

All scriptural examples help us understand this second function of the anatomy of love: love reveals. In doing so, it is more powerful than any darkness. In every aspect of its synonyms, truth, light, and love, this remains consistent: they destroy darkness, lies, and fear.

Truth

John 8:31–32—*"If you abide in My word [continually obeying My teachings], you are truly My disciples. And you will know the truth, and the truth will set you free."*

Love

1 John 4:18—*"There is no fear in love. But perfect (complete, full-grown) love drives out fear…"*

Light

John 1:5—*"The Light shines on in the darkness, and the darkness did not understand it or overpower it."*

- **To Reveal to Heal**

Because we understand the function of love through the lens of Jesus, we know something extremely important: the mechanism of love operates as a two-way street of restoration. This is the path, *"The Way,"* that we are called to follow. When God reveals, it is to heal. When God heals, He will also reveal.

Everywhere Jesus went, His actions exemplified this dual function. He was revealing to heal; He was exposing the truth of someone's spiritual or physical condition. And He was healing to reveal; He was restoring them so that the truth of who they really were—their redeemed identity—could appear.

Because truth, love, and light are synonyms, they share the same objective: to expose darkness, lies, and fear. The purpose is not to shame you, but decisively to free you.

Think of a doctor's visit. When you walk into a hospital, the doctor asks you a list of questions. That process reveals the truth of your symptoms. By revealing the truth, the doctor can provide the right care. It is the same with God. Truth always reveals to heal, and healing always reveals truth.

To Direct – *"I Am the Way"* Jesus

Jesus is the ultimate, living demonstration of *"the Way"* back to the Source. Without this tangible reference point, direction becomes just an abstract concept. Through Jesus, it becomes a concrete reality.

God's sole, driving purpose is to bring you back to Him. He has sacrificed significantly to establish a system that guarantees you the choice to return. Your willingness to draw near to Him affects everything around you, because you become a part of that directional system.

The mission of Jesus is to be the perfect bridge between God and us. As you approach Jesus, His tangible presence begins to direct, shape, and realign your life. In that alignment, others are naturally drawn closer to Him as well. Is this not the essence of discipleship? You follow Him, and your following inherently becomes a direction for others.

Your ministry is meant to be a natural extension of the overflowing love you have for God. It expresses itself through service and loving your neighbor as yourself. But if you pursue ministry without first pursuing who God is—which is love—you will inevitably fall. You will fall because love is the fundamental guiding path that takes you home.

Every time you choose to walk in love, it actively directs you closer to your true self, the one God created. How does it direct you? It is by His Spirit, the very Essence of love itself. His Spirit is a path, a spiritual GPS, that always and unfailingly points to God.

Jesus said, *"I am the Way."* If Jesus is the Way, and God is Love, then love itself carries the inherent direction—which is Jesus. Love has movement. It leads. It pulls you into alignment with divine purpose. Love directs your choices, refines your motives, purifies your intentions, and brings you into deeper intimacy with God.

Why? Because love originates from Him and is perfectly designed to return you to Him.

Love is not soft, weak, or passive. Love is the most aggressive and undefeated force in the entire spiritual realm. Love resurrects what the enemy tried to bury in despair and death. Love heals what demons attempt to break through sickness and trauma. Love reveals what darkness tried to hide with lies and deception. Love directs your steps when confusion tries to derail your destiny.

This is precisely why Satan fights love so violently. Love dismantles every single weapon formed against you. When you live in love, you live in God. When you live in God, the enemy loses all jurisdiction over your life.

As we close Chapter 1, *"Knowing God,"* understand this foundational truth: spiritual warfare is not primarily a battle against demons. It is fundamentally a battle of identity against the identity demons want you to adopt.

The believer who is rooted in the Supreme, supernatural, multidimensional, resurrecting, truthful, healing, revealing, and guiding love that is God cannot be conquered. Love is the war strategy that wins every single time.

As we transition out of this first chapter, remember that God stands outside of time. He is above, beyond, and before all created things. Truth belongs entirely to Him. The force that aligns you with this Supreme, multidimensional, supernatural Entity is one of the most effective weapons you possess. It is the core strength of your spiritual man.

I have only laid the ground here. The Holy Spirit Himself will expand and deepen this revelation as you spend time with God. Now we can move forward into the next effective weapons against the devil.

Chapter 2 — The Colors of The Holy Spirit: The Breath, The Wind, And The Fire

How can we put into words the immense beauty of the Holy Spirit? He is our Helper, Comforter, and so much more. To explain His multifaceted nature, I want to use a metaphor that has profoundly touched my heart: *The Colors of the Holy Spirit.*

Just as colors cannot be confined to a single shade, neither can the Holy Spirit. Every day reveals a new dimension of His power, presence, and love. The golden warmth of His comfort, the deep blue of His deliverance, the fiery red of His conviction—each of these colors represents an encounter waiting to happen. Which *"color"* do you need to experience more fully in your life today? Colors are how my spirit recognizes His movements before my mind can fully explain them.

The Dynamic Ruach: Who is the Holy Spirit?

The Holy Spirit is often described in terms that defy easy definitions: unseen, powerful, and life-giving. The Hebrew word *ruach* provides a key to unlocking this mystery. It is a single word encompassing *wind*, *breath*, and *spirit*. This dynamic imagery reveals the very essence of God. He is a force that cannot be contained or predicted—only experienced. Scripture does not treat *ruach* like a theory; it shows *ruach* in motion.

From the very beginning, the *Ruach Elohim* was active. In the formless void before creation took shape, *"the Spirit of God was moving (hovering, brooding) over the face of the waters"* (Genesis

1:2). Like a mighty, unseen wind, the Spirit swept across the chaos, bringing order and potential. Where the Spirit hovers, chaos stops being final.

This same *"wind"* appears throughout Scripture. At the global flood, God *"made a wind [ruach] blow over the land, and the waters receded"* (Genesis 8:1). At Pentecost, the arrival of the Spirit was heralded when *"a sound came from heaven like a rushing, violent wind, and it filled the whole house"* (Acts 2:2). This wind-dimension of the Spirit moves nations, calms storms in our lives, and signifies God's powerful presence and intervention. The same wind appears again and again because God repeats Himself until we recognize Him.

Beyond the powerful wind, the *ruach* is the intimate breath of God that animates all life. Genesis 2:7 illustrates this: *"Then the LORD God formed man from the dust of the ground, and breathed into his nostrils the breath of life; and the man became a living being [an individual complete in body and spirit]"* (Genesis 2:7). This divine breath is what separates humanity from mere matter. It is the spiritual essence that connects us to our Creator and gives us a living soul. Without His breath, we are bodies. With His breath, we are beings.

Ruach Ha-Kodesh (the Holy Spirit) is the presence of God dwelling within His children. It is the very same Spirit that resided in Yeshua (Jesus) and now lives in every believer. As Scripture tells us, *"If anyone does not have the Spirit of Christ, he does not belong to Him"* (Romans 8:9). Galatians 4:6 reminds us that because we are sons and daughters, God has sent the Spirit of His Son into our hearts, enabling us to cry out, *"Abba! Father!"* Under the New Covenant, the Ruach Ha-Kodesh is no longer merely around you— He comes to live within you.

If we want to understand how the *ruach* operates in real time— how wind, breath, and Spirit function together—we find one of the clearest demonstrations in Ezekiel 37. Ezekiel's vision is perhaps the most potent illustration of the Spirit's power to breathe life into the dead, revealed in the valley of dry bones. The prophet saw a seemingly hopeless situation become an *"exceedingly great army"* through the power of God's command and the infusion of His breath (*ruach*). Scripture records God commanding the prophet to call the breath from the four winds to *"breathe on these slain, that they may live"* (Ezekiel 37:9–10).

The Spirit in Motion — How Ruach Operates

Ezekiel 37 reveals the precise process of the Spirit's operation. Within a single chapter, we see the *Ruach* move in distinct phases, each one necessary for life to return. This vision shows that the Spirit does not operate in only one way or capacity. Instead, He moves progressively, intentionally, and in perfect order—demonstrating that restoration is both structured and alive.

Here, we observe the different movements of the Spirit within that single chapter, each revealing a specific function of *ruach* in action.

Guidance and Transport (v. 1):

"The hand of the LORD was upon me, and carried me out in the spirit of the LORD, and set me down in the midst of the valley which was full of bones…"
In this first movement, the *Ruach* acts as a transportive wind. The Spirit moves the prophet both physically and spiritually, positioning him precisely where ministry must take place. Before restoration can begin, the Spirit brings God's servant to the right location and perspective.

Observation and Revelation (v. 2–3):

"He led me back and forth among them... He asked me, 'Son of man...'"

Here, the Spirit guides Ezekiel's perception. He causes the prophet to observe carefully, to see fully, and then to engage in dialogue. The pivotal question—*"Can these bones live?"*—initiates a moment of faith. The Spirit defines the reality of the situation while simultaneously inviting human agreement with divine possibility.

Command and Prophecy (v. 4–6):

"Then He said to me, 'Prophesy to these bones and say to them... I will make breath enter you, and you will come to life.'"

In this phase, the *Ruach* supplies exact words. Human speech becomes empowered with divine authority. The Spirit does not bypass Ezekiel's voice; He fills it. This reveals a key principle: God's Spirit often chooses to work through yielded human obedience rather than apart from it.

Creative Power (v. 7–8):

"As I was prophesying, there was a noise, a rattling sound, and the bones came together, bone to bone... tendons and flesh appeared on them, and skin covered them..."

Here, the *Ruach* operates in pure creation. Structure forms. Order is restored. Yet, life has not entered. This moment reveals a sobering truth: form without breath is still incomplete. Restoration can appear outwardly finished while still lacking true life.

Resurrection Life (v. 9–10):

"Prophesy to the breath... This is what the Sovereign LORD says: Come, breath, from the four winds and breathe into these slain, that they may live."

This final movement releases resurrection life. The breath enters, and what was assembled becomes alive. The *Ruach* now functions in its fullest expression—turning restored bodies into *"an exceedingly great army."* This is not mere revival; it is mobilization.

The same Spirit who moved over the waters at creation, filled the upper room at Pentecost, and breathed life into dry bones still moves today. He is not waiting to be defined, categorized, or limited. He is waiting to be encountered.

One Substance, Three Persons

We can use a simple yet powerful analogy to grasp the Holy Spirit's place within the Godhead: water, ice, and vapor are all H_2O. They exist in different forms, yet they remain the same substance. In the same way, the Father, the Son, and the Holy Spirit are distinct—not three gods, but one God—revealed in three Persons.

This truth is essential. The Trinity is not a division of essence, but a unity of substance expressed through relational distinction. Each Person operates uniquely, yet never independently. They share the same nature, the same authority, the same divine essence.

The Holy Spirit, in particular, is a presence so vast and multifaceted that any attempt to confine Him to a single theological *"box"* will always fall short. Scripture consistently reveals the immense breadth of His ways, showing Him to be both intimate and infinite—personally present, yet cosmically powerful.

Just as the *Ruach* manifested in diverse movements and dimensions throughout Ezekiel's vision, the Holy Spirit expresses Himself across a wide spectrum of identity and power. He moves as breath, as wind, as fire, as presence, and as life—never contradicting Himself, yet never limiting Himself to one expression.

This is why the Holy Spirit cannot be reduced to a function, a feeling, or a moment. He is God in motion—fully divine, fully personal, and fully active within creation and within the believer.

The Colors of the Holy Spirit

I use a metaphor inspired by my artistic background: **"The Colors of the Holy Spirit."** I remember the encounter I had with the darkness as a child. I vividly recall the feeling, the color, and even the sound of it. That memory is etched into me.

But when I consciously encountered the Holy Spirit for the first time—meaning I knew it was Him—I remember seeing a beautiful sunset color in my grandmother's church. It was overwhelming. I began crying uncontrollably, not out of fear, but because I knew I was safe. It was the first time I felt free to stop holding back my pain.

Every time I opened my eyes, all I could see was that beautiful orange dancing in the room. Worship itself became a color, a glow. It carried the scent of freedom—something that transfixed my soul and broke chains deep within me. I can never forget that moment or what I saw.

As a creative person with open spiritual eyes, I sometimes perceive the world in spectrums and shades, often divided into two categories: good and evil. This way of seeing allows me to simplify complex realities and express them in accessible terms. This metaphor is precious to me. It keeps me in a posture of wonder, where I am simply waiting to encounter a new color each day. I pray it becomes precious to you as well.

A color is an expression, and an expression is a color. Through this lens, I want to present the Holy Spirit by observing His expressions throughout biblical chronology. We will do this so you can reconcile with a vital truth: the Holy Spirit is far greater than you may have imagined.

Remember, Satan does not want you to see God for who and what He truly is—and he certainly does not want you to see the Holy Spirit clearly. This timeline will organize the activity of the Holy Spirit sequentially, from eternity past to eternity future, revealing His continuous and active involvement throughout all of history.

The Holy Spirit Through Time — His Continuous Work

Before Time & Creation

He existed before the beginning. The Holy Spirit is eternal, uncreated, and fully God. Before time existed, He was.

> *"In the beginning the Word already existed. The Word was with God, and the Word was fully God. He was present with God in the beginning. All things were made through Him, and apart from Him nothing was made that has been made"* (John 1:1–3).

He formed and conceived Jesus with His attributes before anything was created. Before creation, the Spirit carried the nature and essence of Christ, revealing the eternal unity within the Godhead.

> *"The Spirit of the LORD will rest on Him—the Spirit of wisdom and understanding, the Spirit of counsel and strength, the Spirit of knowledge and the fear of the LORD"* (Isaiah 11:2).

In Creation and Sustenance

Creation was done through Him. The Holy Spirit was the active agent in the beginning, bringing order out of chaos. The opening lines of Genesis powerfully describe this action:

"The earth was formless and void [a waste and emptiness], and darkness was upon the face of the deep [the primeval ocean that covered the unformed earth]. The Spirit of God was moving (hovering, brooding) over the face of the waters" (Genesis 1:2).

It was His movement that initiated order.

Creation was accomplished with Him and is governed by Him. Every system of creation—light, seasons, laws, and order—was formed with His participation and is sustained by His governance. We see the delicate hand of the Spirit in the cosmos:

"By His Spirit He adorned the heavens; His hand pierced the fleeing serpent" (Job 26:13).
This same power continues to uphold all things.

He breathed into Adam's nostrils the breath of life. Humans obtained living souls when the Spirit entered man. This intimate act of creation signifies that life itself is a spiritual endowment from God.

"Then the LORD God formed man from the dust of the ground and breathed into his nostrils the breath of life; and the man became a living being [an individual complete in body and spirit]" (Genesis 2:7).

Creation functions because of Him. Life continues, grows, and moves because the Spirit sustains all that was created. His ongoing breath is the source of all life we see around us.

"The Spirit of God has made me, and the breath of the Almighty gives me life" (Job 33:4).

It is by sending forth His Spirit that the face of the earth is renewed (Psalm 104:30).

A unique portion of Him was given to humanity to function within creation. We carry His imprint—creativity, dominion, imagination, and the capacity for relationship—reflecting the image of the Triune God. This divine likeness is our origin point:

"Then God said, 'Let Us make man in Our image, according to Our likeness'... So God created man in His own image" (Genesis 1:26–27).

Throughout the Old Testament

He provides empowerment for leadership and craftsmanship. In the Old Testament, the Spirit temporarily equipped individuals for specific divine tasks, empowering both leaders and creatives to fulfill their assignments. We see this with Bezalel, whom God filled with the Spirit to design the tabernacle:
"I have filled him with the Spirit of God in wisdom and skill, in understanding and intelligence, in knowledge, and in all kinds of craftsmanship" (Exodus 31:3). He also clothed Gideon (Judges 6:34) and came mightily upon David (1 Samuel 16:13) for leadership.

He offers prophetic inspiration. Through the prophets, the Spirit revealed God's will, warnings, promises, visions, and direction.

"For no prophecy was ever made by an act of human will, but men moved by the Holy Spirit spoke from God" (2 Peter 1:21).

He gives new hearts and a new spirit. God promised an internal work of the Spirit under the New Covenant to enable genuine obedience and a deep relationship with Him. This was something the old law could not fully achieve. This future reality was prophesied by Ezekiel:

"Moreover, I will give you a new heart and put a new spirit within you... I will put My Spirit within you and cause you to walk in My statutes, and you will keep My ordinances and do them" (Ezekiel 36:26–27).

His wind moves throughout Scripture. The Hebrew word *Ruach* signifies God's powerful and dynamic intervention in both the physical and human realms. His movement shifts nations, breaks cycles, and ushers in divine intervention. He dried the floodwaters with His breath:

"And God made a wind [ruach] to pass over the earth, and the waters subsided" (Genesis 8:1).

That same ruach returned at Pentecost as a *"rushing violent wind, and it filled the whole house"* (Acts 2:2).

He empowers judgment and the destruction of evil. The Spirit's power is not only comforting; it is also a *consuming fire* that brings divine justice against sin and opposition to God:

"For our God is indeed a consuming fire" (Hebrews 12:29). *And again, "For the Lord your God is a consuming fire; He is a jealous (impassioned) God [demanding what is rightfully and uniquely His]"* (Deuteronomy 4:24).

This was dramatically demonstrated when God's fire consumed Elijah's sacrifice on Mount Carmel. Scripture says:

"Then the fire of the LORD fell and consumed the burnt offering and the wood, and even the stones and the dust; it also licked up the water in the trench" (1 Kings 18:38).

And in the judgment that followed:

"Elijah said to them, 'Seize the prophets of Baal; do not let one of them escape.' So they seized them; and Elijah brought them

down to the brook Kishon, and [as God commanded] he slaughtered them there" (1 Kings 18:40).

He also empowered Samson's destructive acts against the Philistines. *"The Spirit of the LORD came upon Samson mightily..."* (Judges 14:6). Later, *"The Spirit of the LORD came upon him mightily, and he went down to Ashkelon and killed thirty men of them..."* (Judges 14:19). When the Philistines tried to bind him, *"The Spirit of the LORD came upon him mightily, so that the ropes on his arms were like flax that had burned with fire... He found a fresh jawbone of a donkey..., and with it he struck down a thousand men"* (Judges 15:14–15).

And finally, in his last act of judgment, Samson prayed, *"O Lord GOD, please remember me and please strengthen me just this time..."* (Judges 16:28). Then, *"Samson leaned with all his strength... and the house fell on the lords and on all the people... So the dead whom he killed at his death were more than those whom he killed during his life"* (Judges 16:29–30).

In the Life of Jesus on Earth

He gave birth to the Messiah. The Spirit miraculously caused the virgin conception of Jesus in Mary's womb, a unique supernatural act.

"And the angel answered and said to her, 'The Holy Spirit will come upon you, and the power of the Highest will overshadow you; therefore, also, that Holy One who is to be born will be called the Son of God'" (Luke 1:35).

He led and inspired the ministry of Jesus. Jesus' entire ministry relied entirely on the Spirit's power and guidance, setting an example for all believers. His mission statement revealed this reliance:

"The Spirit of the Lord is upon Me, Because He has anointed Me to preach the gospel to the poor; He has sent Me to heal the brokenhearted, To proclaim liberty to the captives and recovery of sight to the blind, To set at liberty those who are oppressed" (Luke 4:18).

The Holy Spirit in the Individual Believer

He was released at Pentecost. After Jesus' ascension, the Spirit was poured out permanently on believers, fulfilling Old Testament promises and establishing the Church. This moment shifted His presence from resting temporarily upon people to dwelling within them.

"And they were all filled with the Holy Spirit and began to speak with other tongues, as the Spirit gave them utterance" (Acts 2:4).

He empowers us with Himself. The Spirit gives believers divine power to be witnesses of Christ, equipping them with boldness, conviction, authority, and supernatural endurance. This is a core promise for every follower of Jesus:

"But you shall receive power when the Holy Spirit has come upon you; and you shall be witnesses to Me... to the end of the earth" (Acts 1:8).

The Holy Spirit Governing the Church

He forms and directs the Church. The Holy Spirit actively guides the Church's missions, leadership, and growth, as recorded throughout the Book of Acts. He is the ultimate strategist for the Body of Christ. *"As they ministered to the Lord and fasted, the Holy Spirit said, 'Now separate to Me Barnabas and Saul for the work to which I have called them'"* (Acts 13:2).

He gifts us with tools for His expression. The Spirit's gifts are supernatural manifestations through believers for ministry and edification. These diverse gifts are all expressions of the same divine source:

"There are diversities of gifts, but the same Spirit" (1 Corinthians 12:4).

The following lists detail the specific expressions and operations of the Holy Spirit active in the Church today:

The 9 Gifts of the Spirit (1 Corinthians 12:8-10)	The Fivefold Ministry Gifts Given by Christ (Ephesians 4:11)
Word of Wisdom	
Word of Knowledge	Apostles
Faith	Prophets
Gifts of Healing	Evangelists
Miracles	Pastors
Prophecy	Teachers
Distinguishing between Spirits	
Speaking in Different Kinds of Tongues	
Interpretation of Tongues	

The Fruit of the Spirit

(Galatians 5:22-23)

These represent the divine nature expressed through our transformed lives, the character of Christ developed within us:

Love – *agapē.*

Literal meaning: Selfless, unconditional, sacrificial love; the highest form of love that seeks the good of others without expecting anything in return.

Spiritual significance: God's own love poured into your heart. It protects, nurtures, and restores relationships.

Joy – *chara.*

Literal meaning: Inner gladness or delight; a deep-seated gladness independent of circumstances.

Spiritual significance: A settled gladness rooted in God's presence, not external events; it strengthens your spirit.

Peace – *eirēnē.*

Literal meaning: Wholeness, completeness, inner calm; harmony with God and others.

Spiritual significance: Peace is the tranquility of the soul and stability in relationships; it's the absence of inner conflict.

Patience / *Long-suffering – makrothumia.*

Literal meaning: The ability to endure suffering, delay, or provocation without anger or resentment.

Spiritual significance: Perseverance and restraint under pressure; the Spirit teaches you endurance.

Kindness – *chrēstotēs.*

Literal meaning: Moral excellence, goodness toward others, helpfulness, compassion.

Spiritual significance: Acts of love expressed in gentleness and generosity toward others.

Goodness – *agathōsynē.*

Literal meaning: Uprightness of heart and life; virtue; integrity.

Spiritual significance: Doing what is morally right; the Spirit makes your character reflect God's nature.

Faithfulness – *pistis* (sometimes included instead of meekness).
Literal meaning: Loyalty, trustworthiness, reliability.

Spiritual significance: Being dependable in your walk with God and in relationships; steadfastness.

Gentleness / *Meekness – prautēs.*
Literal meaning: Strength under control; humility, mildness of spirit.

Spiritual significance: Power tempered with humility; the ability to respond softly rather than harshly.

Self-control – *enkrateia.*
Literal meaning: Mastery over one's desires and impulses; discipline.

Spiritual significance: Living in restraint, not dominated by cravings, passions, or fleshly desires.

He teaches us about Himself, about love, about truth, and about our identity. The Spirit is a personal Helper and teacher, forming Christ's character within us (the Fruit of the Spirit) and interpreting God's will to our hearts.

Jesus promised: *"But the Helper, the Holy Spirit... He will teach you all things, and bring all things to your remembrance what I said to you"* (John 14:26).

He helps us understand His ways, His tools, and our purpose. He provides insight and guidance, leading us into truth and revealing God's plan and clarity in confusion. He is our constant, reliable guide:

"However, when He, the Spirit of truth, has come, He will guide you into all truth; for He will not speak on His own authority, but whatever He hears He will speak; and He will tell you things to come" (John 16:13).

He intercedes for us with groanings too deep for words. When believers struggle to pray or to articulate their needs, the Spirit intercedes on their behalf in accordance with God's perfect will. Romans 8:26 beautifully explains:

"Likewise, the Spirit also helps in our weaknesses. For we do not know what we should pray for as we ought, but the Spirit Himself makes intercession for us with groanings which cannot be uttered."(Romans 8:26).

He makes us whole in love so we can continue Jesus' mission. The Spirit's presence results in holy character and love (the Fruit of the Spirit), empowering believers to represent Christ's mission with purity and power. This character has grown internally through His work:

"But the fruit of the Spirit is love, joy, peace, longsuffering, kindness, goodness, faithfulness, gentleness, self-control" (Galatians 5:22–23).

He seals us for the day of redemption. The Spirit is a divine seal and guarantee of our future inheritance and eternal life. He marks us as God's own, securing our place in the kingdom. Ephesians 1:13 says believers were:

"Sealed with the Holy Spirit of promise, who is the guarantee of our inheritance." (Ephesians 1:13)

The End of the Age
He will be the final voice calling humanity to Christ. At the end of time, the Spirit works through the Church (the Bride) to offer the

final invitation to salvation. Revelation 22:17 captures this final call to humanity:

"And the Spirit and the bride say, 'Come!' And let him who hears say, 'Come!' And let him who thirsts come. Whoever desires, let him take the water of life freely." (Revelation 22:17)

Why Satan Minimizes The Holy Spirit

I could go into more depth… but I am trying to help you *see* the Holy Spirit. Do you know that He has a far bigger place than the one we usually give Him? Yes, in church we see Him as a Helper, and that's true. But do we really understand what the word **"Helper"** means?

To help effectively, one must possess what the one in need does not. A true Helper carries access, insight, and power that exceed the capacity of the one receiving help. Help does not come from lack—it comes from abundance.

The Holy Spirit is called the Helper because He supplies what humanity cannot produce on its own: power, wisdom, discernment, endurance, and life. A Helper is never deficient; a Helper operates from fullness.

This does not disrupt divine order. God remains the Head—the source of authority. Jesus is our Shield and Mediator—the covering through whom access is granted. And the Holy Spirit is the Helper—the One who executes, empowers, and applies what the Father has willed, and the Son has secured.

This divine structure mirrors the order God established in marriage. Scripture calls the wife a *"helper,"* not because she is lesser, but because she carries strengths, capacities, and insight the husband does not possess. Headship and help are not measures of value—they are expressions of function.

In the same way, the Holy Spirit is not lesser because He helps. He helps because He has more to give in the realm of power and execution. He does not replace the Head, nor override the Shield— He makes their work effective in us.

So why do we minimize Him? Why do we treat the Holy Spirit like He's optional, or like He's just a comforter for moments of need, instead of the One who actually knows everything? Why don't we choose to follow the One who holds all power, wisdom, and authority?

This minimization is precisely what the enemy wants. He doesn't want you to connect with the Holy Spirit fully. He doesn't want you to realize that your connection to Him is a weapon, because the Holy Spirit is connected to everything. He is the breath of life, the fire of God, the wind that moves nations. He is the power that raises the dead.

Your connection to the Holy Spirit is your source, your power, your strategy, and your guidance. When you walk with Him, you are walking connected to the only One who knows all things, sees all things, governs all things, and will complete all things.

The Holy Spirit is not small or secondary. He is God. Fully God. Eternal God. The God who lives in you. If you will yield to Him, follow Him, and open yourself fully, you will discover power, wisdom, love, and victory that you can't get anywhere else.

Chapter 3 — Knowing Jesus — The Man, The Image, And The Blood

PART I — THE MAN AND THE IMAGE

One of the most effective weapons in spiritual warfare is truly knowing Jesus. And to *know* Him means more than just learning facts about His life. It means intimacy. To know someone is to spend time with them intentionally. It means to choose to be alone with them and to invest in understanding their heart. Without that investment, knowledge remains incomplete.

That is why Scripture must be approached as a relationship, not information. The goal is not to "get through" the text, but to let the text bring you into proximity with a Person.

When you read the epistles, you are not simply reading stories. You are receiving lifetimes of testimony in a single passage. The genealogies, lists of names, and even the seemingly tedious details carry hundreds of years of life experience. Skipping them means missing wisdom that could save your life. And this is before we even consider the Spirit's inspiration behind those writings. The point is, Jesus is worth the time and focus.

And the more time you spend with Him, the more you realize that Jesus cannot be reduced to a historical figure. His story is not merely human—it is divine invasion. His life is the visible expression of an eternal reality.

Jesus' origin is not of this earth. His conception in Mary was a supernatural act in time, but His existence is eternal, co-eternal with the Father before creation. This is not a story of human origin, but of the eternal God stepping into the temporal. With Him, He brought power, authority, and life that nothing in this world can replicate.

In the previous chapter, we mentioned that one expression of the Holy Spirit was the conception of Jesus. Scripture does not describe biological mechanics, but it does reveal the spiritual blueprint of the Messiah. Etymologically, the word *"conceive"* comes from the Latin verb *concipere*. Concipere means "to take in, receive, or seize." It is formed by combining two parts:

"Con-": a prefix meaning *"with"* or *"together."*
"Capere": a verb meaning *"to take"* or *"seize."*

So, to *conceive* literally meant "to take in" or "to receive" something. Over time, it came to mean "to form a concept or idea." It also came to mean "to become pregnant," the idea of receiving and nurturing life. Conceiving can also describe being formed with a group of ideas or final concepts that can be embedded in your DNA, behavior, and talents.

Regarding Jesus, these "final ideas" can be understood as the attributes of the Spirit that conceived Him. These qualities reveal who the Messiah is, not how His biology functioned. This links His eternal character to the prophecy in Isaiah 11:1–2, which says:

"Then a Shoot (the Messiah) will spring from the stock of Jesse [David's father], and a branch from his roots will bear fruit. And the Spirit of the Lord will rest on Him…"

The Spirit of **Wisdom**
The Spirit of **understanding**
The Spirit of **counsel**
The Spirit of **strength**
The Spirit of **knowledge**
The Spirit of the [reverential and obedient] fear of the Lord.

So, when we ask, "conceived by what?" The answer is found in these attributes: the **Spirit of the Lord with wisdom, understanding, counsel, might, knowledge, and fear of the Lord**. While the Bible does not explicitly call these "seven spirits," this is a common interpretation that links the eternal qualities of Jesus with the Spirit's work in Him.

Mary's womb (Luke 1:35) was the site of a miraculous and supernatural act by the Holy Spirit. The revelation in Isaiah helps explain what was supernaturally planted in Mary's womb. As the Holy Spirit overshadowed her, the conception of Jesus was a fully supernatural act of God, accomplished by the Holy Spirit through divine overshadowing.

In Section V of the book "Demonology 101," Chapter 3, the grouping of demons, I introduced you to the concept that the spirit is a personality. If spirits have personality, then the Spirit who conceived Jesus reveals His personality most clearly. That study is consistent even for Jesus.

If He was conceived by the sevenfold Spirit of God, then by studying the character traits of these spirits, we can draw out Jesus' character and behavior traits, which is His true image and radiance. He is the one we have to know, recognize, mirror, and follow—in our cognitive behavior, and much more.

PART II — A SPIRIT IS A PERSONALITY: TRAITS, COGNITION, AND FRUIT

In psychology, a personality trait is a stable pattern of behavior, thought, or emotion that forms a unique personality. Psychology provides names for these patterns, but spiritually, we know the deeper reality behind them. Our core assertion in spiritual warfare is this: **persistent traits often reveal spiritual influence, and**

personality can become the seat of a stronghold—the "strong man" (Matthew 12:29).

This means that personality is not neutral. It is not merely a psychological preference or temperament. It is often the visible expression of an invisible authority operating beneath the surface.

Traits are external expressions of internal spiritual realities. The consistent, stable personality we observe is often a stronghold, or the "strong man" (Matthew 12:29), empowered by a group of cooperating spirits. Psychology uses models such as the Big Five personality traits—Openness, Conscientiousness, Extraversion, Agreeableness, and Neuroticism—to map human personality. Psychology describes patterns; Scripture reveals roots. I use both, but I submit both to Christ.

These dimensions display consistent clusters of traits that mirror the grouping of spirits. For example, Neuroticism manifests as anxiety, fear, worry, moodiness, and sadness—traits that cluster predictably. Spiritually, this cluster might be identified as "spirits of fear" or "spirits of depression." Low Agreeableness involves traits such as manipulation, hostility, apathy, and selfishness, all hallmarks of "Jezebel" or "Belial"-type influences.

When a deliverance minister observes these consistent clusters of traits, they are not merely identifying a psychological pattern. They are identifying the signature of a specific type of spirit or group of spirits. The persistence and severity of these traits—often exceeding normal human variation—suggest a non-human origin. Just as the Holy Spirit manifests a clear set of fruits—*love, joy, peace, kindness, and self-control* (Galatians 5:22–23)—negative traits also reveal the fruits and nature of darkness.

A Personal Blueprint: Mirroring Christ's Image

We are about to break down the Seven Spirits of the Lord into traits, cognition, and behavior. For each Spirit, I will use the same map: traits, internal cognition, external behavior, and the fruits that confirm what is growing. This entire framework is more than a theological exercise I just created. This is literally how my brain processes and recognizes the image of Jesus in different aspects of life.

I created this detailed template of traits as a personal, internal diagnostic tool. By systematically comparing my behavior, thoughts, and emotional responses to the perfection of Christ's character, as recorded in Scripture, I can measure my spiritual growth. I can then identify the areas where I am still operating out of old "strongholds" rather than under divine influence.

At the beginning, this concept was just for my personal journey. I said I created it, but the truth is that the Holy Spirit created it in me. It was a private way to make sure I was actually following Christ and not fooling myself. As I began to encounter false prophets, deceptive spiritual practices, and even psychopathy and pedophilia inside the church, this concept became a vital safety filter that the Holy Spirit forged in my brain and intellect.

I have spent so many years taking the beams out of my own eyes in the presence of the Holy Spirit. He led me to confront my own patterns. I stayed long enough to observe the roots of my reactions, and now the Holy Spirit has trained me to see patterns in others—from the fruit all the way back to the root. He has shown me this all in full love and compassion. There is no need to judge when you are too busy looking at the origin of things.

The process happens very fast. Sometimes it feels almost mathematical, like a formula, and the final result I look for is always Jesus. If the result isn't Jesus, the Holy Spirit immediately begins to break down the situation in my mind, showing me which spirit is actually operating. He does this through a voice of Scripture or a picture. When I confront the person with the truth He revealed, the accuracy is always confirmed, and the healing is imminent.

This framework gives me an objective standard: Do the actions, the words, and the character of this person reflect the image of Christ and His traits?

What amazes me is that this concept continues to renew itself. It grows, it overlaps with other revelations, and its consistency proves itself every time I spend time with God. He also teaches me that some fruits take time to develop—not time as we measure it on earth, but the "time currency" of transformation. The burning, the refining, and the surrender determine the rate of change, not the clock in the sky.

I will develop this entire concept further in another book because it deserves a deeper exploration. But for now, this is the foundation we will use as we break down the Seven Spirits of the Lord in the following sections. Jesus does not merely possess these traits—He embodies them.

PART III — THE SEVENFOLD SPIRIT: THE IMAGE OF CHRIST BROKEN DOWN

1. The Spirit of the Lord (Ruach Yahweh)

Identity & Definition

The Spirit of the Lord is the overarching Spirit of God Himself, the foundation of Jesus' identity as God incarnate. This Spirit establishes divine authority, moral integration, and sovereign identity. Psychologically, this represents the perfectly integrated self: a core identity defined by ultimate authority and a complete moral constitution. This unity forms the sovereign personality and the integrated moral self.

Personality Traits (Who He Is)

Divine — expressing ultimate authority, presence, and completeness; functioning from identity rather than insecurity.

Whole — a cohesive, internally integrated self marked by emotional stability, harmony, and unified purpose.

Holy — resisting corruption and pursuing moral excellence in thought, motive, and action.

Integrity — remaining truthful, consistent, and aligned with moral truth in every circumstance.

Sovereign — exercising internal mastery over impulses, emotions, and decisions; ruling oneself before ruling others.

Authoritative — guiding others through legitimacy, moral clarity, and truth rather than force or fear.

Just — committed to righteousness, fairness, and moral equity without compromise.

Compassionate — perceiving suffering accurately and responding with restorative action.

Loving *(Agape)* — expressing unconditional, sacrificial love aimed at the highest good of others.

Internal Graces (What He Cultivates Within)

This Spirit cultivates identity before action. When the Spirit of the Lord governs a believer, He forms the internal foundation that makes all other spiritual growth possible.

Submission to divine authority
Alignment with God's will
Identity rooted in truth rather than performance
Moral clarity
Self-governance before external leadership

How Fruit Is Formed (Process, Not Performance)

"But the fruit of the Spirit [the result of His presence within us] is love [unselfish concern for others], joy, peace, patience [not the ability to wait, but how we act while waiting], kindness, goodness, faithfulness." — Galatians 5:22 (AMP)

The *gift* of the Holy Spirit produces *fruit*. There are different categories of spiritual gifts, all originating from the Holy Spirit— from inherent talents we are born with to the empowerment we receive upon receiving the Spirit. Here, I am not referring only to the gifts of expression, but to the internal gifts that help us navigate and cultivate our soul, affecting our personality and eventually empowering our outward expression. These are all intrinsically linked to the fruits mentioned in Galatians 5:22.

I appreciate the word *"result"* in the Amplified translation because it implies practical discipline and repetition. I also love the word *"fruit,"* because it signifies something that grows under a cycle; each tree cycles differently, and not all fruit bears at the same time.

When the Holy Spirit dwells within you, He comes with His full personality—His gifts. In every situation, He invites your soul to make a decision: *"Use My gift."* When you choose Him, you are actually choosing to be led by Him.

As you engage with Him internally, something is produced externally—not immediately, but progressively, as you continue choosing to be led. These actions become activated and visible in your life, leaving an imprint not only on your behavior but also on your neural pathways. This happens because repeated choices affect your brain chemistry and create a natural response. That cognitive response is the fruit. These gifts you partner with begin to reshape your inner world, producing new patterns of thought, new ways of processing experiences, and ultimately forming a sovereign, Spirit-led personality.

Cognitiveness (How This Spirit Thinks — Internal Fruit)	Behavior (How This Spirit Acts — External Expression)
Thinks from identity, not reaction.	Acts with calm authority rather than domination.
Perceives reality without distortion or insecurity.	Leads without fear or insecurity.
Recognizes divine order, authority, and hierarchy.	Corrects injustice decisively and righteously.
Processes situations calmly from truth rather than emotion.	Protects truth and righteousness.
Understands moral boundaries clearly.	Moves with confidence rooted in identity, not reaction.
Operates from eternal perspective rather than urgency or fear.	Demonstrates compassion through action, not sentiment

Fruits That Multiply in Believers:

When this Spirit governs a believer, the following fruits become visible over time:

Love — the foundation of God's nature expressed through the believer.

Peace — inner stability rooted in divine authority.

Integrity — consistency between inner life and outward action.

Holiness — attraction toward purity and separation from corruption.

Stability — emotional and spiritual steadiness under pressure.

Moral courage — the strength to stand for truth regardless of cost.

Self-control — mastery over impulses and reactions

Jesus Embodied the Spirit of the Lord

Jesus perfectly demonstrated the Spirit of the Lord throughout His life and ministry. His authority was revealed when He rebuked the wind and waves, bringing immediate calm (Mark 4:39). He exercised righteous justice when He cleansed the temple, confronting corruption without hesitation (John 2:15–16). His compassion was evident as He looked upon the crowds and was moved to heal and restore them (Matthew 9:36). Ultimately, His love was displayed in laying down His life for His friends (John 15:13).

Jesus ruled first over Himself, then over creation, sickness, sin, and death. The Spirit of the Lord governed His identity, thoughts, actions, and authority. He is the perfect expression of **Ruach Yahweh**, the foundation Spirit from which all other expressions flow.

2. The Spirit of Wisdom (Ruach Chokmah)

Identity & Definition

The Spirit of Wisdom imparts divine strategy, heavenly intelligence, and the ability to navigate life with precision. It forms the mental architecture of a godly personality, the part of you that learns to think like God, recognize patterns, solve problems with clarity, understand systems, and discern the right path in complex situations. Psychologically, this reflects higher cognitive functioning, emotional intelligence, and the integration of truth with action.

Personality Traits (Who This Spirit Is)

Insightful — a mind trained to see beneath the surface; perceiving root causes, patterns, consequences, and hidden motives with clarity.

Strategic — able to organize information, foresee outcomes, and select the most effective course of action; combining foresight with discernment.

Discerning — the capacity to distinguish between truth and deception, wisdom and foolishness, divine influence and counterfeit voices.

Prudent — able to make thoughtful, measured decisions; responding rather than reacting; weighing long-term implications before acting.

Sound-minded — stable in judgment, emotionally regulated, and cognitively balanced; thinking clearly under pressure without distortion.

Teachable — open to correction, instruction, and growth; not defensive, not rigid, but flexible in truth and anchored in humility.

Creative — able to receive innovative divine solutions; perceiving possibilities and pathways others cannot see.

Orderly — mentally structured, organized, and intentional; bringing clarity out of chaos and direction out of confusion.

Internal Graces (What This Spirit Cultivates Within)

Patience in decision-making
Humility to receive instruction
Clarity under pressure
Submission of intellect to divine truth
Dependence on God's perspective rather than personal logic

Gifts That Cultivate This Personality (1 Corinthians 12 — formed through close proximity to the Holy Spirit)

Word of Wisdom — the Spirit-given ability to apply God's purpose and plan to specific situations with precision and timing.

Word of Knowledge — supernatural revelation of facts about people, circumstances, or spiritual realities that could not be known naturally.

Prophecy — perceiving God's mind and intention and establishing it in the present through direction, strategy, or ordered steps toward victory.

Discernment of Spirits — the ability to identify the true source behind thoughts, influences, and environments, whether divine, human, or demonic

Cognitiveness (How This Spirit Thinks — Internal Fruit)

Thinks in patterns rather than moments, seeing the long arc of God's plan.

Processes information from divine perspective rather than emotional reaction.

Recognizes the difference between impulse and instruction, desire and destiny.

Understands consequences before actions are taken.

Measures decisions against God's truth before responding.

Identifies spiritual influences shaping situations and people.

Breaks down complex problems with calm, structured thinking.
Reasons from identity rather than insecurity, from truth rather than trauma.

Holds multiple perspectives without confusion and integrates them into clarity.

Behavior (How This Spirit Acts — External Expression)

Speaks with clarity, accuracy, and restraint.
Make decisions slowly, intentionally, and prayerfully.

Brings order, strategy, and direction into chaotic environments.

Avoids impulsive reactions and emotional decision-making.

Guides others through wisdom rather than pressure.

Build solutions instead of escalating conflict.

Fruits That Multiply in Believers

Clarity — freedom from confusion and double-mindedness.
Peace — calm confidence rooted in trust in God's direction.
Patience — the ability to wait without anxiety or frustration.
Self-control — mastery over impulses, emotions, and reactions.
Discernment — accurate judgment without suspicion or pride.
Stability — consistency of thought and action under pressure.

Jesus Embodied the Spirit of Wisdom

Jesus demonstrated the Spirit of Wisdom throughout His life and ministry. He silenced traps without defensiveness, answered questions with divine precision, and revealed God's truth without escalation. He discerned hearts instantly, understood timing perfectly, and acted only in alignment with the Father's will. His wisdom was deliberate, measured, and sovereign—never rushed, never reactive.

Through Him, we see **Ruach Chokmah** expressed in perfect clarity and peace, revealing divine intelligence lived out in human form.

3. The Spirit of Understanding (Ruach Binah)

Identity & Definition

The Spirit of Understanding brings deep comprehension, empathy, and clarity to the heart and mind. It forms the internal framework for relating rightly to God, people, and circumstances with insight, sensitivity, and perceptive wisdom. This Spirit allows truth to move from information into internalized understanding. Psychologically, this reflects emotional intelligence, relational depth, and the capacity to process and integrate truth for righteous action.

Personality Traits (Who This Spirit Is)

Insightful — able to grasp underlying principles, motives, and spiritual realities beyond surface appearances.

Empathetic — sensing and resonating with the emotions, struggles, and needs of others, responding with compassion.

Disciplined — emotionally and mentally steady; regulating responses in alignment with truth and moral integrity.

Open-minded — receptive to multiple perspectives and willing to adjust understanding when aligned with God's truth.

Analytical — able to break down complex situations, interpret patterns, and integrate information accurately.

Reflective — pauses to meditate on experiences, revelations, and truth before acting.

Loving (*Agape*) — expressing unconditional care, warmth, and sacrificial commitment to the highest good of others.

Just — committed to fairness, righteousness, and moral equity; refusing exploitation or oppression.

Patient — willing to give time and space for understanding, growth, and unfolding transformation.

Perceptive — attuned to subtle spiritual cues, emotional signals, and hidden dynamics often overlooked.

Internal Graces (What This Spirit Cultivates Within)

Emotional maturity
Relational wisdom
Compassion rooted in truth
Patience in understanding people and processes
Sensitivity without emotional instability
Discernment guided by love

Gifts That Cultivate This Personality (1 Corinthians 12 — received through proximity to the Holy Spirit)

Word of Knowledge — supernatural revelation of facts about people, circumstances, or spiritual realities not known naturally.

Prophecy — perceiving God's mind and intention and establishing it in the present through direction, clarity, and righteous alignment.

Discernment of Spirits — the ability to distinguish the true source behind thoughts, influences, and environments, whether divine, human, or demonic.

Cognitiveness (How This Spirit Thinks — Internal Fruit)

Processes information with depth and nuance rather than surface reaction.

Integrates spiritual truth with human experience.

Perceives motives, intentions, and emotional needs accurately.

Considers long-term relational and spiritual consequences of actions.

Balances compassion with righteous judgment.

Thinks strategically about relationships, decisions, and moral outcomes.

Remains calm, focused, and discerning under pressure.

Reflects God's perspective in thought patterns and conclusions.

Behavior (How This Spirit Acts — External Expression)

Acts with empathy and clarity in interpersonal interactions.

Responds thoughtfully rather than impulsively.

Guides others with understanding, encouragement, and truth.

Interprets complex emotional and spiritual situations accurately.

Applies correction or support with wisdom and compassion.

Creates safe spaces for growth, healing, and understanding.

Fruits That Multiply in Believers

Compassion — love expressed through understanding and action.

Patience — endurance with people and processes without frustration.

Peace — emotional stability rooted in clarity and trust in God.

Kindness — gentle, thoughtful engagement with others.

Discernment — accurate perception guided by love rather than suspicion.

Emotional maturity — stability in response and relationship.

Jesus Embodied the Spirit of Understanding

Jesus consistently demonstrated the Spirit of Understanding in how He related to people. He perceived hearts, motives, and wounds with precision and compassion. He responded to brokenness without condemnation and confronted deception without cruelty. He understood suffering, betrayal, and weakness, yet remained anchored in truth. His interactions revealed deep emotional intelligence guided by divine understanding. Through Him, we see perfect comprehension balanced with perfect love.

4. The Spirit of Counsel (Ruach Etsah)

Identity & Definition

The Spirit of Counsel provides divine guidance, strategy, and direction. It forms the internal compass for decision-making, problem-solving, and navigating life in alignment with God's will. This Spirit governs how conclusions are reached and how solutions are formed according to truth. Psychologically, it reflects strategic judgment, integrated reasoning, and the ability to guide cognition, emotion, and action toward righteous outcomes. Where psychology seeks understanding and resolution, the Spirit of Counsel becomes the divine source of true guidance and direction.

Personality Traits (Who This Spirit Is)

Guiding — leading others with clarity, precision, and spiritual insight rooted in truth.

Strategic — thinking with foresight, recognizing long-term outcomes, and planning steps aligned with God's purposes.

Discerning — accurately identifying the nature of situations, motives, and the appropriate course of action.

Supportive — providing counsel, encouragement, and wisdom that strengthens confidence and capacity in others.

Influential — inspiring others to follow righteous paths without coercion or control.

Patient — willing to wait for God's timing while preparing, mentoring, and guiding faithfully.

Decisive — making firm, righteous decisions grounded in moral clarity and divine insight.

Adaptable — adjusting approach and strategy without compromising truth or integrity.

Internal Graces (What This Spirit Cultivates Within)

Confidence in God's direction
Wisdom in leadership and mentorship
Clarity in decision-making
Stability under pressure
Humility in offering counsel
Discernment rooted in truth

Gifts That Cultivate This Personality (1 Corinthians 12 — received through proximity to the Holy Spirit)

Word of Wisdom — Spirit-given insight to apply God's purpose and plan accurately in specific situations.

Prophecy — perceiving God's intention and establishing it in the present through direction, alignment, and strategic steps.

Word of Knowledge — revealing divine principles and insight that guide understanding and action.

Gifts of Healing — restoring clarity, soundness, and wholeness in those struggling, enabling righteous decisions.

Cognitiveness (How This Spirit Thinks — Internal Fruit)	Behavior (How This Spirit Acts — External Expression)
Thinks in alignment with God's purposes rather than human impulse.	Provides guidance that is accurate, timely, and strengthening.
Evaluates options carefully, weighing moral alignment and consequence.	Leads others by example, modeling wisdom, patience, and integrity.
Discerns patterns, motives, and spiritual dynamics within situations.	Resolves conflict with justice, tact, and spiritual insight.
Plans with foresight, strategy, and divine order in mind.	Acts with authority rooted in truth, not force or fear.
Processes relational and circumstantial information accurately.	Offers correction and encouragement in ways that promote growth.
Balances counsel with compassion, offering guidance without judgment or bias.	Demonstrates calm, intentional decision-making even in chaos.
Remains focused, clear-headed, and stable under pressure.	Maintains ethical consistency and moral clarity in leadership roles.
Integrates wisdom, discernment, and insight into every conclusion.	Creates environments of trust, clarity, and alignment with God's will.

Fruits That Multiply in Believers

Peace — inner and relational stability that inspires confidence and trust.

Patience — the ability to guide, mentor, and wait effectively.

Kindness — thoughtful actions rooted in insight and care.

Goodness — decisions that reflect moral excellence and ethical wisdom.

Faithfulness — reliability and consistency in guidance and leadership.

Self-control — mastery over impulsive reactions, ensuring measured responses.

These fruits reveal that strength is growing, manifesting as empowered, Spirit-driven endurance in your life.

Jesus Embodied the Spirit of Counsel

Jesus consistently demonstrated the Spirit of Counsel through His guidance of the disciples. He gave strategic instructions for ministry and conflict (Matthew 10:1–4). He responded to accusation and moral failure with insight and redemptive wisdom (John 8:1–11). He discerned timing through prayer and alignment with the Father (Mark 1:35). He counseled His followers with foresight, preparing them for spiritual trials and growth (Luke 22:31–32). Through Him, we see divine counsel expressed with clarity, authority, and love.

5. The Spirit of Strength (Ruach Geburah)

Identity & Definition

The Spirit of Strength provides divine capacity for endurance, power, and resilience. It forms the internal reservoir of courage, perseverance, and spiritual fortitude, enabling the overcoming of opposition and adversity. This Spirit empowers decisive action under pressure while maintaining moral and spiritual integrity. Psychologically, it reflects emotional resilience, willpower, and the ability to remain steady and effective in conflict, delay, pain, and resistance.

Personality Traits (Who This Spirit Is)

Courage — the mental and spiritual capacity to face danger, difficulty, or opposition with steadfast resolve.

Resilience — the ability to recover from setbacks while maintaining stability and strength.

Fortified — inner strength that sustains righteous action despite suffering or resistance.

Persevering — committed to mission and purpose, remaining steady through trials.

Confident — secure in God's provision and alignment, able to act without fear.

Enduring — sustained effort and patience while pursuing righteous goals.

Empowered — able to draw upon divine energy to influence circumstances constructively.

Bold — acting decisively in alignment with truth without recklessness.

Internal Graces (What This Spirit Cultivates Within)
Spiritual stamina
Courage under pressure
Resilience after failure or setback
Steadiness in trial
Self-mastery in conflict
Righteous endurance in obedience

Gifts That Cultivate This Personality (1 Corinthians 12 — received through proximity to the Holy Spirit)

Faith — supernatural certainty in God's character and promises, producing confidence beyond visible evidence.

Working of Miracles — manifestations of God's power that overcome natural limitations and opposition.

Gifts of Healings — restoration and strengthening for the wounded and weary, producing renewed capacity and resilience.

Word of Wisdom — divine insight into the best course of action for victory, endurance, and righteous momentum.

Cognitiveness (How This Spirit Thinks — Internal Fruit)

Assesses challenges with clarity and confidence in God's strength.

Evaluates risk and opposition without fear, relying on divine power.

Forms strategic responses grounded in wisdom, justice, and spiritual principles.

Maintains focus and perseverance toward goals despite obstacles.

Integrates spiritual and practical understanding to sustain long-term effort.

Think proactively, anticipating opposition and preparing accordingly.

Balances boldness with obedience, courage with prudence.

Trusts God's timing and provision while remaining active and engaged.

Behavior (How This Spirit Acts — External Expression)

Acts with decisive courage in challenging situations.

Endures trials with steadfast faith and resilience.

Protects and supports others through strong, steady leadership.

Demonstrates perseverance in ministry, work, and personal growth.

Responds to opposition with righteous action and spiritual authority.

Upholds justice and righteousness even when challenged.

Maintains integrity under pressure, staying consistent with truth.

Exhibits boldness without arrogance and strength without domination.

Helps others rise through difficulty with practical empowerment.

Fruits That Multiply in Believers

Love — sacrificial concern even under pressure.

Holiness — purity and ethical alignment in adversity.

Peace — calm steadiness and inner composure in trial.

Patience — sustained endurance over prolonged challenges.

Kindness — using strength to support and uplift others.

Goodness — applying power to righteous and constructive outcomes.

Faithfulness — loyalty and steadfast commitment despite resistance.

Self-control — restraint and discernment in provocation and pressure.

These fruits reveal that strength is growing, manifesting as empowered, Spirit-driven endurance in your life.

Jesus Embodied the Spirit of Strength

Jesus perfectly embodied *Ruach Geburah* in the wilderness temptation. After forty days of fasting and physical weakness, He exercised extraordinary spiritual fortitude and self-mastery. Every attack from Satan was met with precise, truth-rooted resistance, not emotional reaction (Matthew 4:1–11). He remained steady under pressure, refused compromise, and chose obedience over relief. His courage was quiet, His endurance was intentional, and His strength was governed by holiness. In that wilderness, Jesus revealed what it looks like when divine strength becomes a personality: unwavering endurance, disciplined decisions, and righteous power under pressure.

6. The Spirit of Knowledge (Ruach Da'at)

Identity & Definition

The Spirit of Knowledge provides divine understanding, discernment, and insight. It forms the internal capacity to perceive truth, comprehend spiritual realities, and apply divine principles accurately. This Spirit governs *what is known and how truth is recognized.* Psychologically, it reflects intellectual clarity, analytical reasoning, and the ability to integrate knowledge into action aligned with God's will, while remaining submitted to divine revelation.

Personality Traits (Who This Spirit Is)

Intelligent — demonstrating deep comprehension of the integrity of a thing; understanding beyond surface appearance.

Curious — maintaining a holy desire to explore, question, and understand God's truth and creation.

Perceptive — noticing patterns, motives, and underlying realities others overlook.

Discerning — distinguishing truth from error, light from darkness, substance from illusion.

Analytical — evaluating situations with clarity, logic, and precision without distortion.

Wise — applying knowledge practically to solve problems and make righteous decisions.

Observant — attentive to details that reveal God's patterns and purposes.

Insightful — understanding complex spiritual and human dynamics accurately and deeply.

Internal Graces (What This Spirit Cultivates Within)

Love for truth
Intellectual humility
Clarity of perception
Submission of knowledge to God
Accuracy in judgment
Sensitivity to spiritual reality

Gifts That Cultivate This Personality (1 Corinthians 12 — received through proximity to the Holy Spirit)

Word of Knowledge — Spirit-given revelation of hidden truths, people, circumstances, and realities not known naturally.

Discernment of Spirits — identifying spiritual sources behind thoughts, behaviors, and environments, whether divine, human, or demonic.

Teaching — communicating understanding in ways that clarify, instruct, and guide others into truth.

Word of Wisdom — applying revealed knowledge to produce righteous outcomes and sound decisions.

Cognitiveness (How This Spirit Thinks — Internal Fruit)

Thinks with clarity, integrating divine insight into decision-making.

Analyzes situations precisely, perceiving spiritual and human dynamics.

Recognizes patterns, relationships, and consequences accurately.

Applies knowledge practically, aligning choices with God's will.

Detects deception, error, and hidden motives without suspicion or pride.

Processes complex information while maintaining moral and spiritual integrity.

Thinks critically and strategically while remaining dependent on revelation.

Balances intellect with humility, acknowledging God as the source of truth.

Behavior (How This Spirit Acts — External Expression)

Acts with informed discernment and precise judgment.

Provides guidance and instruction rooted in truth and understanding.

Evaluates circumstances thoroughly before responding.

Makes decisions that reflect both divine truth and practical wisdom.

Identifies and addresses deception or spiritual misalignment accurately.

Share knowledge to teach, strengthen, and build others.

Applies insight to influence outcomes justly and constructively.

Maintains integrity by aligning knowledge, thought, and behavior.

Upholds justice and righteousness through accurate understanding.

Fruits That Multiply in Believers

Love — care guided by understanding and truth.
Holiness — purity of thought, motive, and action.
Peace — clarity and stability in thinking and interaction.
Patience — calm discernment before response.
Kindness — using insight to benefit and guide others.
Goodness — applying knowledge toward righteous outcomes.
Faithfulness — reliability and devotion to truth.
Self-control — restraint and discipline in thought, speech, and action.

These fruits reveal that divine knowledge is maturing and manifesting as accurate, Spirit-led wisdom in life.

Jesus Embodied the Spirit of Knowledge

Jesus perfectly embodied *Ruach Da'at*. He discerned the motives of the Pharisees and crowds, perceiving the intentions behind their questions and actions (Matthew 22:15–22). He revealed deep spiritual truths to His disciples, guiding them into understanding through the Spirit of truth (John 16:13). He interpreted and applied the Law with perfect accuracy, revealing its true intent and fulfillment (Matthew 5:17–20). He consistently recognized deception and spiritual influence, addressing them with clarity and authority (Luke 6:6–10). In every encounter, Jesus demonstrated complete spiritual awareness, showing how a life aligned with God's Spirit navigates truth, error, and instruction with precision and integrity.

7. The Spirit of the Fear of the Lord (Ruach Yirah)

Identity & Definition

The Spirit of the Fear of the Lord establishes reverence, awe, and submission toward God. It forms the internal foundation for humility, obedience, and moral alignment, anchoring the soul in an accurate awareness of God's holiness and authority. This Spirit governs *why* we choose righteousness even when no one is watching. Psychologically, it reflects self-regulation, moral awareness, and a deeply rooted recognition of one's position before divine authority, guiding behavior through conscience, respect, and accountability.

Personality Traits (Who This Spirit Is)

Reverent — maintaining profound awe and respect for God's nature, order, authority, and presence; prioritizing Him before thought and action.

Humble — recognizing personal limitations and fully submitting to God's power, wisdom, and authority.

Obedient — willingly aligning decisions and actions with God's commands and eternal principles.

Pure — living with moral and spiritual integrity, cultivating transparency and honesty before God.

Disciplined — exercising control over impulses, emotions, and desires in alignment with God's will.

Conscientious — maintaining constant awareness of ethical and spiritual responsibility.

Respectful — honoring God's order, creation, and delegated authority.

Devout — fully committed to worship, prayer, and communion with God as the center of life.

Internal Graces (What This Spirit Cultivates Within)	Gifts That Cultivate This Personality (1 Corinthians 12 — received through proximity to the Holy Spirit)
Holy reverence Moral sensitivity Humility before God Submission of will Accountability of conscience Desire for holiness	Speaking in Tongues — deepening communion with God and heightening spiritual awareness beyond natural language. Interpretation of Tongues — bringing spiritual understanding to what God communicates in the spirit. Prophecy — receiving and declaring God's heart, instruction, and correction with clarity. Discernment of Spirits — cultivating awareness of God's will and detecting compromise or deception in complex situations.

Cognitiveness (How This Spirit Thinks — Internal Fruit)

Thinks with continual awareness of God's presence and authority.

Evaluates decisions based on moral and spiritual alignment rather than convenience.

Consider ethical consequences and eternal accountability.

Prioritizes God's will above personal desire, comfort, or preference.

Remains vigilant against spiritual deception and moral compromise.

Processes experience through humility, awe, and responsibility.

Balances courage with obedience in decision-making.

Applies reverence strategically to guide relationships, leadership, and conduct.

Behavior (How This Spirit Acts — External Expression)

Lives in consistent obedience and submission to God.

Maintains ethical integrity privately and publicly.

Demonstrates humility in leadership and interpersonal relationships.

Responds to challenges with reverence, discernment, and restraint.

Exercises disciplined self-control in speech, thought, and action.

Encourages others to honor God through example and instruction.

Lives transparently with purity and accountability.

Acts decisively while honoring divine order and authority.

Fruits That Multiply in Believers

Love — compassion guided by reverence and obedience.

Holiness — moral and spiritual purity in every area of life.

Integrity — alignment of thought, speech, and action with God's will.

Justice — promoting righteousness and fairness through godly restraint.

Peace — inner calm rooted in trust and submission to God.

Patience — disciplined endurance through trials and correction.

Kindness — humility and care expressed toward others.

Goodness — obedience producing righteous outcomes.

Faithfulness — loyalty to God's commands and purposes.

Self-control — restraint and discernment governed by reverence for God.

These fruits reveal that the fear of the Lord is maturing, producing a life anchored in holiness, wisdom, and obedience.

Jesus Embodied the Spirit of the Fear of the Lord

Jesus perfectly embodied **Ruach Yirah**. He lived in complete submission to the Father, surrendering His will entirely to God's purpose, even unto death on the cross (Philippians 2:8). He acted only in alignment with what He saw the Father doing, demonstrating total dependence and reverence (John 5:19). His life was marked by disciplined prayer, devotion, and obedience, withdrawing regularly to commune with God (Luke 5:16). In every word and action, Jesus honored the Father, revealing a soul fully governed by reverential fear. Through Him, we see that the fear of the Lord is not terror, but holy alignment that produces obedience, wisdom, and life.

The true beauty of this process is not that it is complicated, but that it is effective. Each time you choose to be led by the Spirit, something is reinforced within you. Over time, what began as a conscious decision becomes your natural posture. This is identity formation. Through this process, you also begin to recognize Jesus more clearly in every situation, as a living standard by which everything else is measured.

Jesus modeled this reality perfectly. His power did not come from force, charisma, or domination, but from obedience rooted in love. He did not resist the Father's will or attempt to reshape it; He remained aligned with it. That alignment was His authority. Darkness could not move Him because He was anchored in complete surrender—and surrender to God is never weakness.

Through this kind of Spirit-led repetition, the Holy Spirit establishes the spiritual man within you. Your mind is renewed, your responses are recalibrated, and your inner structure is rebuilt in the image of Christ. What once required effort begins to happen instinctively. What once felt like restraint becomes your default nature, not because you are forcing change, but because you are being transformed.

The result is not theoretical. You become a living testimony. Your presence carries weight because it reflects alignment, not performance. You become a strategic force in the spiritual realm— not by striving to fight darkness, but by walking in obedience that displaces it. Darkness recognizes alignment and retreats from it. The power of a transformed heart is not loud or chaotic; it is steady, grounded, and immovable.

This is the strength of a soul that has fully surrendered. This is the simplicity of a warrior who cannot be shaken. This is the life Jesus lived—and it is the life we are called to walk.

PART IV — THE BLOOD OF JESUS: THE COVENANT WEAPON

The Blood Is Relationship Before It Is Warfare

Before we speak about the blood of Jesus as a weapon, we must first recognize that it is a relationship. In the previous section, we encountered Jesus as the Man, the Image, and the embodiment of obedience. The blood does not stand apart from Him; it is the extension of who He is. The blood carries His life, His obedience, and His covenant authority. What Jesus lived in the body, the blood now speaks in the spirit. Without knowing Jesus, the blood becomes a formula. But when Jesus is known, the blood becomes authority.

The blood of Jesus is the most potent and frequently invoked weapon in the Christian arsenal against the devil. Jesus Himself secured our victory through this sacrifice. Yet a critical shortfall remains: many within the Christian community do not fully trust the power of the blood because they lack a foundational understanding of what it actually is. Many Christians do not know *why* it works. That lack of knowledge opens the door to false protections, including those proposed by witchcraft. This is not a failure of desire, but a failure of knowledge.

Why Many Christians Don't Trust the Blood

Many believers invoke the blood faithfully, yet without revelation. When power is used without understanding, trust weakens. Where trust weakens, substitutes appear. Witchcraft does not succeed because it is stronger; it succeeds because it offers explanations where the Church has often offered repetition without illumination.

The laws of atonement and the magnitude of Christ's sacrifice are often misunderstood or inadequately taught. Yet when a witch doctor asks someone to purchase an animal for sacrifice, it makes sense to the human mind because the law of blood is being acknowledged. To engage in actual spiritual warfare, these truths must be clarified. There is no authentic spiritual victory without *"the blood that speaks better things"* (Hebrews 12:24). Therefore, we must understand the integrity of the blood.

To understand why the blood of Jesus works, we must return to a foundational principle that governs everything God creates. Nothing in the Kingdom functions by mystery alone. Power flows from design, and design flows from God. When we understand the integrity of a thing, why it exists, how it was designed, and what order governs it, we gain access to its authority. The blood of Jesus is no exception.

The Integrity of a Thing: Identity, Purpose, Order

The integrity of a thing is the discovery of why a thing or a being exists through the lens of God. It is uncovering the truth according to God, not according to man. When we pursue the integrity of a thing, we discover its design in three dimensions.

The first dimension is identity, or name. This answers the question: *What is it by design?* This is not merely what people call it, but what the Creator declares it to be. In Scripture, God names things according to their nature and origin, as demonstrated in Genesis 1.

The second dimension is purpose, or assignment. This answers the question: *Why does it exist?* Everything God creates is released with a function. In Genesis 1:11, when God commanded the earth to bring forth vegetation, that command was its assignment. In the same way, when God called you into existence, His voice established your function.

The third dimension is order, which produces wholeness and goodness. This answers the question: *How is it meant to operate?* Biblical integrity implies internal consistency between belief, character, and action (Proverbs 11:3). It means functioning within divine order (Proverbs 21:3), which produces good fruit and reflects God's declaration that creation was "very good" (Genesis 1).

PART V — THE INTEGRITY OF BLOOD: IDENTITY, PURPOSE, ORDER.

To approach the blood of Jesus correctly, we must first settle the question of *what blood is by God's definition.* Scripture does not introduce blood as a substance first, but as a witness. The first mention of blood appears in Genesis 4:10, after Cain murders his brother Abel: "*The Lord said, 'What have you done? The voice of your brother's innocent blood is crying out to Me from the ground for justice.'*

Blood is introduced with a voice before its function is explained. This tells us something essential: blood does not simply circulate life — it speaks life. It carries identity, memory, and legal standing in the spirit realm.

The Hebrew word used here for blood is דָּם *(dam),* meaning "blood" or *"life-fluid"*. Embedded in this word family is the story of humanity itself. אָדָם *(Adam)* means man. אֲדָמָה *(adamah)* means ground. Man was formed from the ground, animated by breath, and sustained by blood. Language itself ties man, earth, and blood together.

In Genesis 4:10, the word blood appears in its plural form, *demey* (*"bloods"*). According to ancient Jewish teachings, this does not refer only to Abel's physical life, but to every life that would have flowed from him. Cain not only murdered his brother; he silenced a generation.

This reveals blood nature as God names it: blood carries life beyond the individual. It holds lineage, inheritance, and destiny.

Here is the core revelation: **blood is spirit in liquid form**. It bears witness. It testifies. Abel's blood cried out without a mouth, without lungs, without language. God heard it because blood speaks in the realm of law.

God never contradicts Himself between the spiritual and the natural. What Scripture reveals in the unseen, the body confirms in form. Biology does not redefine blood; it echoes what God already established.

Blood enters the body through the order in the natural realm. Life begins with the meeting of seed and soil; the mother's egg functions as the soil, carrying nutrients and half of the genetic code. The father's sperm functions as the seed, holding the other half. When they unite, a zygote forms with a complete blueprint of forty-six chromosomes. This blueprint is DNA.

DNA is a biological instruction. It is the **voice that tells life how to take shape**.

Blood and DNA function together. Blood is life in liquid form. DNA is the voice of that life, declaring what the body is designed to become before the body ever exists. *"For the life of the flesh is in the blood"* (Leviticus 17:11).

Once the blueprint is established, the multiplication begins. The zygote multiplies into an embryo, and DNA acts as the command center, telling every cell what to become. Between days 18 and 21, the yolk sac produces the first blood cells. Weeks later, a heart tube forms and starts beating, pumping those early cells. The liver then takes over blood production, and eventually, the bone marrow becomes the permanent factory. Every phase confirms the spiritual reality that the blueprint precedes the building, and the voice determines the form.

The blood in your body is created through the voice of your DNA (DNA CODE). **The blood in your veins is older than you are in physical form.** This fact makes the plural *demey* ("bloods") in Genesis 4:10 make a lot of sense.

The Purpose of Blood: Life, Lineage, Witness, Atonement, Covenant

A. Life is in the Blood.

Blood is spirit in liquid form, and it precedes structure. Because of this, the primary function of blood is to sustain both physical and spiritual life.

Blood is the life force that flows through the body. DNA is the voice of that blood, the internal code that declares what the body is designed to look like, carry, and become because the blood in your veins is older than you are in physical form (Leviticus 17:11).

B. The Bloodline Carries Identity and Inheritance.

Because blood carries life that precedes you, it logically acts as a biological archive. DNA is imprinted with memories that carry generational patterns, which can manifest as either blessings or curses. Confronting and breaking these deep-seated patterns requires spiritual authority and intentionality. As Jesus taught concerning stubborn spiritual opposition:

"However, this kind [of demon/pattern] does not go out except by prayer and fasting" (Matthew 17:21).

The combined practice of prayer and fasting is a spiritual mechanism for addressing these inherited patterns.

When we fast, the body enters a state of **lethargy** and begins to break down stored energy. Science even shows that fasting can initiate cellular repair (autophagy) and, surprisingly, may influence gene expression and reset certain DNA patterns.

Spiritually, as the body weakens, the spirit grows stronger. The discipline of fasting and prayer brings us into profound alignment with God. This divine alignment allows His Spirit to confront and destroy not only the demonic influence attached to a bloodline, but also the very patterns written in the flesh, our DNA, and our genome.

C. The Blood Bears Witness.

Blood testifies before God. As we discussed in Section One, in modern forensic science, we have begun to "hear" that voice using different means. We analyze blood at a crime scene to determine the sequence of events and how the crime was committed. We also use DNA testing to identify the specific individual involved.

It is amazing to see that the blood was always bearing witness; humanity has simply just started listening, and today, technology has evolved to catch up on that revelation.

D. The Blood Requires Atonement (Bringing Life Back).

Atonement literally translates to *"at-one-ment,"* meaning to reconcile or make amends. Since blood represents life, when sin causes death or separation from God, a payment of blood must answer for it. This is a universal spiritual law that many people are not aware of:
"And according to the law, almost all things are purified with blood, and without shedding of blood there is no remission [forgiveness]" (Hebrews 9:22).

In the Old Covenant, the blood of animals temporarily covered sin. In the New Covenant, the perfect blood of Jesus permanently cleanses us and releases us from sin and its guilt:

"For the life of the flesh is in the blood, and I have given it to you upon the altar to make atonement for your souls; for it is the blood that makes atonement for the soul" (Leviticus 17:11).

E. The Blood Seals the Covenant

Finally, blood functions as the seal of a covenant. Covenants in the Bible were always ratified with blood, symbolizing the binding of two lives together in an unbreakable agreement:

"Then he took the Book of the Covenant and read in the hearing of the people... And Moses took the blood, sprinkled it on the people, and said, 'This is the blood of the covenant which the Lord has made with you according to all these words'" (Exodus 24:7–8).

Jesus established a new and better covenant using His own blood:

"Likewise, He also took the cup after supper, saying, 'This cup is the new covenant in My blood, which is shed for you'" (Luke 22:20).

Once the identity and purpose of blood are understood, order must be addressed.

The Divine Order of Blood: Why Jesus' Blood Alone

The blood of Jesus is the final and ultimate sacrifice toward which everything before it was pointing. To grasp why His blood alone is necessary and sufficient, we must recognize that the Old Covenant functioned as a foundation for the New Covenant. Its laws and practices were never permanent solutions; they were formative instructions, lived rehearsals, preparing humanity for an eternal reality that would be established through Christ. This is why we cannot remain bound to Old Covenant practices that were not explicitly reaffirmed, refined, or fulfilled in Jesus' ministry.

Jesus Himself declared, *"I came to fulfill the Law"* (Matthew 5:17). The Law, the prophecies, the priesthood, and the animal sacrifices were given so the people could be shaped, trained, and made ready. When Jesus arrived, He completed what had been partial and perfected what had been provisional. In doing so, He established the requirements of an eternal covenant and rendered temporary systems obsolete. Practices not restored or transformed through Christ no longer carry authority, because the New Covenant is not transitional; it is final.

There is a decisive distinction between animal blood and the blood of Jesus. One belonged to a period when His blood was not yet accessible. The other belongs to eternity, after the New Covenant was enacted. This distinction is not symbolic; it is legal and spiritual. Yet Satan attempts to construct a parallel system by attaching corrupted wisdom to the law of atonement and the law of blood. The result is a counterfeit framework that resembles truth while quietly undermining it.

Blood is a voice that transcends dimensions. If it did not, God could not hear it. Blood carries spiritual law, including the law of atonement. These laws are real. But when they are detached from covenant, they become exploitable mechanisms rather than instruments of redemption.

PART VI — COUNTERFEITS: OCCULT BLOOD SYSTEMS VS. COVENANT BLOOD

Blood as Currency: The Transactional Lie

From an occult perspective, blood is understood as currency. In that sense, they are not entirely wrong. Blood carries life, and life is perceived as transferable power. But in occult systems, blood is never relational. It is transactional. It is not covenantal; it is contractual.

Occult traditions recognize what Scripture revealed long before them, but they twist its purpose. Yes, blood speaks. Yes, blood pays a price. Yes, the blood voices open access in the spirit realm. But instead of a covenant, occult systems pursue leverage. Blood is used to compel spiritual forces to act in exchange for the release of life. This is why blood rituals appear across cultures and throughout history. Fallen angels taught these practices to humanity.

Whether animal or human, blood is used to seal pacts, empower spells, bind spirits, or manipulate outcomes. Witchcraft is still a covenant, but it is a covenant of darkness. The logic is simple: life is exchanged for power. The greater the life offered, the greater the power expected.

The Hidden Cost: How Blood Contracts Become Bondage

What occult systems refuse to answer honestly is this: **who pays the cost?**

Occult practice does not require faith in God. It operates on the belief that law can be sustained by God's structure without relationship to God's nature. It promises quick gain by pretending accountability does not exist. Precision and ritual accuracy become the measure of success. But this logic collapses when examined across time. Someone always pays for the blood that is shed.

When innocent blood is used as payment for influence, advancement, or protection, it is murder. That blood does not disappear; it testifies. The same legal voice that opens access becomes the argument demons use to kill, steal, and destroy bloodlines across generations. This is how corrupted wisdom functions: spirits lie by omission. They promise power while hiding costs. They never release authority; they extract it. Every occult contract transfers ownership and places a bloodline into servitude. What looks like control is, in truth, bondage.

Why Biblical Sacrifice Is Not Pagan Ritual

Occult practitioners often claim that biblical sacrifice is no different from pagan ritual, insisting that God merely copied ancient traditions. This is false. The law of atonement and occult practice are not the same. One is redemptive and relational; the other is selfish and destructive.

God never instituted sacrifice to manipulate Himself or to teach humanity how to control the spirit realm. Sacrifice was never about forcing divine action. It existed to teach humanity the value of life, the cost of sin, and the necessity of a perfect substitute. Occult practice uses blood to bypass obedience. Atonement, by contrast, exists to restore union with God.

Occult power seeks results without transformation, authority without alignment, and access without surrender. It treats blood as a shortcut. This is why occult power can appear effective in the short term. The law responds. The spirit realm reacts. But the debt is never removed, only delayed. In occult systems, blood always creates obligation. Power must be repaid through repeated sacrifice, generational consequence, or spiritual bondage. Blood in this system never liberates; it binds.

Testimony and Breakthrough: When the Blood Breaks the Cycle

I come from a family where occult practice was present. What I witnessed firsthand was that selfishness always surfaced in decision-making. Even when intelligence was high and spirituality appeared advanced, the conclusions were consistently dark. Wisdom detached from truth produced death.

When a person views their own life as the only life that matters, it reveals a fracture in spiritual intellect. From that place, anything becomes justifiable. Power outweighs people. Results eclipse righteousness. Desire overrides consequence. This is how human sacrifice becomes possible, not suddenly, but progressively. Morality bends. Conscience dulls. Blood becomes currency.

Many are drawn into these systems not for power, but for protection. Desperation invites immediate solutions. When the Church fails to teach the supremacy of the blood of Jesus, people seek answers where answers appear available. I lived this reality. I was born into a bloodline marked by curses because blood was speaking against us. When the Church did not help, desperation led my family back into bondage.

But someone broke the cycle. My grandmother encountered Jesus. Her obedience opened a door to redemption that altered our lineage. Salvation entered where blood contracts once ruled.

PART VII — WHY THE BLOOD OF JESUS SPEAKS BETTER THINGS

Calvary: The Altar of the New Covenant

So, Why the Blood of Jesus? If the law of atonement governs spiritual reality, then blood must speak. The blood of Jesus was shed on Calvary. Calvary became the altar of salvation. That blood established the New Covenant.

The New Covenant does not govern Christians alone; it governs creation itself. It affects angels, humanity, and the dust under your feet. The Loudest Blood: Silencing Curses and Cancelling Claims. If human blood carries ancestral memory, then the blood of Jesus, established before creation, is the oldest blood in existence.

If blood is required to answer for sin, what blood could possibly answer for generations other than the older blood? The blood of Jesus. If human blood is spirit in liquid form, then the blood of Jesus is God in material form, released into the earth to declare victory. When we receive salvation, we participate in His sacrifice by having ourselves nailed to the cross. From this moment, because Jesus' blood is louder than any other blood, because it is an eternal substance, it silences all curses traced and connected to your bloodline. He silences the ransom of sin because He is a greater sacrifice than any blood covenant or blood sacrifice anyone in your bloodline could have ever made. His blood speaks better and more potently because His blood is the origin of all blood.

If animal and human blood can cry out for justice, then it is spiritually coherent that the blood of Jesus speaks better things. If animal blood was only a rehearsal, then the blood of Jesus fully covers the sin of Adam, and by proximity, you and any other life that will be released in this timeline.

If the blood of Jesus is God in liquid form and Jesus is the living Word of God, **then the Word of God is the voice of His blood.** The voice of the spirit that we hear is The Word, the DNA code of His blood.

If occult systems see blood as currency for exchange, then the blood of Jesus can buy back humanity, as He did! His death and resurrection can't be myths or religious fiction. It is a cosmic reality that saves humanity each time they learn about it. It is so genuine and so tangible that it coheres in any reality. It is a legal, spiritual, and an act of rescue, integrity, and love that makes sense in every realm.

Evangelism as Warfare: Don't Shame the Bound—Free Them

Suppose people run to botanicas, voodoo priests, or santeros, satanists, or any occult practice. Christian or not, do you think they would still seek protection elsewhere if they read this revelation? I don't think so, so what are you waiting for? Share the good news about the blood of Jesus!

Spiritual warfare is understanding the blood, the precious blood of Jesus. We do not stigmatize people who run into occult practices; we set them free with the reality of the blood because the blood of Jesus is powerful enough and has already pre-saved anyone who accepts to be saved.

Chapter 4 — Knowing Yourself With The Full Armor Of God

Up to this point, we have identified the weapons. We have studied the enemy's origin, his ministry, his patterns, and his limitations. We have also uncovered the believer's advantage: the covenant, the blood, the Word, the Spirit, and the light. But now we must do something more intimate than learning. We must become.

Spiritual warfare is not meant to remain a collection of concepts you understand. It is meant to become a nature you wear. Many believers know how to pray in emergencies, but they do not know how to live in authority daily. The difference is not intensity. The difference is in formation.

This is why we must end where Scripture ends its warfare instruction: not with a warning, but with a wardrobe. The armor of God is not simply equipment for battle—it is the final stage of spiritual identity. The weapons become clothing. The disciplines become posture. The truths become your reflexes. And what was once an effort becomes your default.

So, in this final chapter, we are not adding a new weapon. We are putting on what we already received. We are stepping into the Ministry of Light fully dressed.

The Armor Is Formation, Not Performance.

This final chapter will not be long. We are simply going to put on the full armor of God with truth, understanding, purity, love, and gratitude. We already know the weapons. Now they become a robe we will never remove. I believe the armor of God is a garment of majesty. It is the gown worn at the wedding of the Lamb. It is the clothing your spiritual man is dressed in when your soul, mind, and strength are filled with light.

To me, spiritual warfare is what Christianity is meant to be. This book is called *Spiritual Warfare*, yes—but more than that, this is what every Christian should understand in order to truly walk as a believer. This is the knowledge required to live a stable, victorious, and fruitful life.

Spiritual warfare is the blood-bought reality of the believer. It is the Christian lifestyle. I know I have revealed some intense truths. You may be reaching this final chapter feeling overwhelmed, asking yourself, *"Am I going to have to fight all my life?"* But when these principles became my natural way of living, I had never been happier, more fulfilled, or more whole. Resisting the devil, discerning God, recognizing the colors of the Holy Spirit, and remaining grateful for Jesus—His nature and His blood—kept my life within the perimeter of God's will and blessing.

I am deeply moved as I write this last chapter. I am thinking about you as you read it. I am writing with tears, because I sincerely pray that this journey blesses you and continues to bless the generations that come after you.

The Ministry of Light: The Domain of Our Arsenal

Our true arsenal operates under an entirely different domain: the Ministry of Light. In the very beginning, God spoke into the void, *"Let there be light,"* and there was light (Genesis 1:3). The Hebrew word used here is אוֹר *('ôr)*, a term that encompasses illumination, brightness, and the very glory of God. Throughout Scripture, this light defines our reality: it is God's presence (Psalm 27:1), His wisdom (Psalm 119:130), the person of the Messiah (Isaiah 9:2), and finally, our own identity as believers (Matthew 5:14).

To truly master our warfare, we must recognize that light is not merely a metaphor; it is a universal law. As the Word declares, *"Light shines in the darkness, and the darkness has not overcome it"* (John 1:5). This is more than a poetic promise—it is a statement of metaphysical reality.

The Law of Absolute Displacement

Consider the simplicity of the physical world around you. Think about the room you are sitting in right now. If you flip a switch and flood that room with light, where does the darkness go? It does not *"fight"* the light. It does not retreat to a corner to plot a counterattack. It is instantly displaced.

In the natural world, science confirms what the Spirit already knows: darkness has no independent existence. You cannot *"turn on"* the dark; you can only remove the light. Darkness possesses no energy, no mass, and no inherent power to extinguish even the smallest candle flame. It exists only in the absence of something greater.

Jesus affirmed this universal law when He declared, *"I am the light of the world. Whoever follows Me will never walk in darkness"* (John 8:12). By identifying Himself as Light, He revealed that His presence functions as the ultimate "light switch" for the human soul.

This is the foundation of the Law of Absolute Displacement. When this law is applied to your life, darkness—whether it takes the form of fear, confusion, or demonic oppression—loses its legal ground to remain. It has no mechanism to "turn off" the light of Christ. Just as a physical room cannot remain dark once the bulb is lit, a life saturated with the Light of the Word cannot remain under the dominion of shadows. Darkness cannot coexist with Light; it must flee.

This is the most crucial realization for the believer: Light represents truth, revelation, purity, healing, and love. Because darkness has no power of its own, it can only occupy the spaces where we have not yet invited the Light. Consequently, wherever the Word of God is revealed and applied, the enemy is not merely defeated—he is expelled.

The reality of our warfare, then, is not a struggle of strength, but a matter of establishment. We win by knowing how to turn on the light, how to become the light, and—most importantly—how to keep the light on.

Covenant Tools: How Light Is Carried

The Law of Light is not a cold or mechanical force; it is embodied in a tangible Person. Jesus Christ is the ultimate, all-effective weapon against the shadows of this age. Because He *is* the Light, the darkness of this world does not merely *"leave"*—it retreats in the face of His legal authority. When Jesus gave Himself, He did not simply offer us a ticket to heaven; He granted us a **Diplomatic Passport** into His system of radiance, giving us legal access to His very divine nature. But how do we practically draw from this power? We do so through specific **Covenant Tools**—the spiritual technology designed to carry His inherent light into the darkest corners of our reality.

The Word (The Frequency of Truth)

This is our source of sanctification. It acts as a spiritual filter, removing the "noise" of the world so we can tune into the frequency of God's truth.

"Sanctify them by Your truth; Your word is truth" (John 17:17).

The Blood (The Legal Coverage)

This is our means of victory. In the courtrooms of heaven, the Blood is the evidence that the debt is paid and the enemy has no claim over us.

"They overcame him by the blood of the Lamb..." (Revelation 12:11).

The Name (The Executive Authority)

The Name of Jesus is the "signature" that authorizes our prayers and commands in the heavenly realms. It is the highest level of clearance available to a believer.

"At the name of Jesus every knee should bow..." (Philippians 2:10).

The Renewed Mindset (The Processing Center)

To walk in light, we must change how we process information, and we process it through the light of God by renewing our minds. That gives us the Mind of Christ; it allows us to see opportunities where the world sees obstacles.

"Let this mind be in you which was also in Christ Jesus" (Philippians 2:5).

The Template for Behavior (The Conduct of Light)

Righteous living is not about following rules; it is about following a pattern of "profitable behavior" that keeps our light-source unobstructed.

"Follow my example, as I follow the example of Christ" (1 Corinthians 11:1).

Jesus brings us into this system through a spiritual legal gateway called the Altar of Salvation, where we are reborn and marked by the waters of baptism.

The Church as Distribution Centers of Light

But the process does not end with our own rescue. Once we are brought into the Light, we are transformed into **Distribution Centers**—the Church.

To ensure that the Light reaches every corner of the earth, Christ equips His representatives—the saints—through the **Five-Fold Ministry**. These are heavenly functions designed to express different dimensions of God's heart:

- **Apostles** carry the *government* of light.
- **Prophets** carry the *voice* and clarity of light.
- **Evangelists** carry the *fire* and reach of light.
- **Pastors** carry the *warmth* and protection of light.
- **Teachers** carry the *structure* and logic of light.

As Ephesians 4:11–12 explains, these gifts were given to *"fully equip and perfect the saints for works of service."* This is the divine strategy: the ministry gifts act as **Master Trainers**, pouring their function into you so that you become a mature, effective vessel of light in your family, your business, and your community.

Jesus did more than provide tools; He gave Himself as the ultimate template for identity. He is the perfect image and flawless reflection of the Father, and we are called to follow that pattern. Spiritual identity is not discovered in isolation—it is formed by imitation. As we yield to Him, we uncover our unique design, a design meant to mirror His radiance.

Here, He reveals a powerful secret: as we navigate these truths in harmony under the guidance of the Holy Spirit, we are crafting something powerful—an armor that we do not merely wear. **We become it.**

Becoming the Armor

The armor of God is not an external uniform you put on before a morning battle brief; it is an internal metamorphosis. It is a wholesome character, a new nature, fully shaped by the Spirit and the Word. The strategic goal remains simple: you keep shining, you maintain the light, and darkness keeps fleeing.

The effective weapons have been defined, and the spiritual laws have been explained. Our mandate is now clear: we must clothe ourselves in the very nature of God. The Apostle Paul lays out the blueprint for this transformation:

"Finally, my brethren, be strong in the Lord and in the power of His might. Put on the whole armor of God, that you may be able to stand against the wiles of the devil..." (Ephesians 6:10–12).

This is not about seasonal changes or temporary battle gear; this mandate calls for divine metamorphosis. While Paul instructs us to *put on* the armor, the Holy Spirit reveals a deeper truth: we are to **become** the armor. We dress ourselves with God Himself, allowing the brilliance of the Holy Spirit to forge an unshakable identity. In this state of being, every piece of the armor radiates a specific frequency of God's nature:

- **Integrity** becomes a light that stops lies from sticking to us.
- **Purity** becomes a light that shields our core processing center from invasion.
- **Peace** becomes a light that radiates outward, creating an impenetrable atmosphere.
- **Focus** becomes a light that reflects and quenches every fiery dart.
- **Mindset** becomes a light that ensures divine clarity and protection.
- **The Word** becomes an offensive laser—the penetrating edge of God's revealed will.

When these virtues mature within you, you are no longer relying on human effort. You are clothed in light itself, embodying the sevenfold Spirit of the Lord (Isaiah 11:2).

The Armor Components: The Active Settings of Identity

To walk in this light, we must understand the mechanical function of each component. These are not merely artifacts of ancient warfare; they are the **active settings of your spiritual identity**.

The Wide Band of Truth

Your Center of Gravity — The Reality: Personal Integrity and Moral Courage.

The waist is your physical center; it provides balance and stability for every move you make. In the spiritual realm, Truth is what holds everything together. If you are not rooted in truth, you will find yourself off-balance in every other area of life.

Truth is not merely information you consume; it is who you are when no one is looking. It is moral courage—the strength to stand firm when the pressure of the world demands that you fold. Without this wide band of truth, your spiritual structure will inevitably collapse under the weight of battle.

The Breastplate of Righteousness

Guarding the Core — The Reality: An Upright Heart in Constant Alignment with God.

This piece protects your heart—the seat of your emotions, your identity, and your decisions. When the heart is exposed, the enemy finds an entry point through shame, lust, pride, or offense.

Righteousness is not a claim to human perfection; it is a relentless commitment to align your heart with God's, even when it costs you. It acts as a spiritual shield for your inner life, ensuring that your core identity in Christ remains untouched by darkness.

The Gospel of Peace

Your Foundation of Stability — The Reality: Firm-Footed Readiness Produced by the Good News.

Your feet determine your direction, and the "shoes" you wear determine your stability. When you strap on the Gospel of Peace, you order your path according to the Good News.

This stability ensures that no matter how chaotic the terrain becomes, you do not drift or stumble. Jesus is the lamp unto your feet and the light upon your path; when your shoes are at peace, you walk through confusion with the steady stride of a victor.

The Shield of Faith

The Deflector of Lies — The Reality: Active Protection Against Fear and Demonic Accusation.

You hold the shield of faith out front to extinguish the "fiery darts" of the wicked one. The enemy hurls arrows of anxiety, doubt, and accusation, but active faith stops them mid-air.

Faith is the realization that the Lord is your fortress, even when your circumstances seem to defy natural evidence. It keeps you covered and immovable while you wait for the manifestation of God's timing.

The Helmet of Salvation

The Mindset of the Saved — The Reality: A Renewed Perspective and a Guarded Mind.

The helmet protects the primary battlefield: your thoughts. Any thought that does not align with Truth is a trespasser on your identity.

Salvation forms a specific, impenetrable mindset. It continually reminds you: *I am not who I used to be. I am not what I feel. I am not what the world says about me.* You are saved, you are covered, and you belong to God. If a thought does not carry the seal of Salvation, the helmet refuses its entry.

The Sword of the Spirit

The Frequency of the Word — The Reality: The Spoken Word of God *(Rhema).*

In the original Greek, the word for *"word"* here is *rhema*, not *logos*. While *logos* refers to the written text, *rhema* is the spoken word. This makes the sword a weapon that lives in your mouth.

You do not fight the enemy with silent thoughts; you fight him with the Word released into the atmosphere. To wield the sword is to declare the promises of God and speak the truth of Scripture aloud. Do not be silent in the heat of battle—your voice is the edge of the blade.

All Prayer and Petition

The Atmosphere of Incense — The Reality: Constant Communion as a Spiritual Climate.

Prayer is the atmosphere that surrounds the entire armor system. When you pray, you burn with the presence of God, creating a cloud of protection.

Without prayer, the armor is merely a costume—it is worn, but inactive. With prayer, the system breathes with power. Your body becomes an altar, and your words rise like fragrant incense before the throne. As Scripture declares, *"Let my prayer be set before You as incense"* (Psalm 141:2).

This *"golden bowl of incense"* (Revelation 5:8) is what keeps your light bright and your armor active. Prayer is the fuel that keeps the fire of the Ministry of Light burning **24/7**.

The Closing Seal: Victory Is Who You Became

If there is one thing I hope you carry in your spirit from this journey, it is this: **victory is not a prize you chase; it is the person you have become**. As we walked through these pages, we didn't simply study the mechanics of darkness—we unmasked its limitations. We looked back at the enemy's origins and the ministry he built on lies, only to realize that his power is a hollow imitation.

We explored the mystery of the blood, realizing that while your human blood carries your story, the Blood of Jesus carries the authority of eternity. We uncovered the *"legal ground"* the enemy uses to trespass, and we discovered the colors of the Holy Spirit— the divine compass that ensures you never lose your way in the shadows. Finally, we looked into the mirror of the Word and saw the truth: **the Armor of God is your true nature—the maturation of Light**.

When truth becomes your spine.
Righteousness becomes your posture.
Peace becomes your steady gait.
Faith becomes your shield.
Salvation becomes the very way you think.
The Word becomes your breath,
And prayer becomes the fragrance you carry into every room.

Spiritual warfare is a lifestyle of continual alignment. When you understand the covenant in the Blood, the enemy loses the right to touch what God has redeemed. When you know the Holy Spirit, darkness loses the right to interpret your life. And when you finally embody the Ministry of Light, hell loses the right to keep you bound.

To walk in this reality, you must first accept the Call, and then accept the Condition. This journey requires an investment of your time and your heart, but the prize at the end of the road is Jesus Himself—and eternal life in His presence.

If you have not yet given your life to Christ, or if you have been wandering in the shadows and desire to step fully into the Light, I invite you to pray this prayer with me now:

"Lord Jesus, I come to You today just as I am. I acknowledge that I have lived in the shadows, and I ask for Your forgiveness. I believe that You are the Light of the World, and that You died and rose again to give me a new identity. I surrender my life to You. Wash me in Your Blood, fill me with Your Holy Spirit, and clothe me in Your Armor. I declare that from this day forward, I belong to the Ministry of Light. Amen."

If you have prayed this prayer, your journey has begun. I encourage you to find a Bible-believing church and seek water baptism. Baptism is the **legal seal of your rebirth**—the moment you publicly exit the kingdom of darkness and enter the system of Light.

My Final Charge to You

We end where we began: with the God who spoke light into existence—and then placed that same light inside of you.

May the God of peace, who through the blood of the eternal covenant equipped you with everything good for doing His will, now work in you what is pleasing to Him. May your armor be bright, and may the light of Jesus that burns inside of you become a burning bush—so consuming that you become a full extension of His mission.

This is not a call to strive harder, but to **shine truer**. You were never meant to merely survive the darkness; you were designed to displace it. Walk clothed in light. Remain anchored in the covenant. Let your life testify that the Light still speaks, still saves, and still transforms everything it touches.

Go forward as one fully dressed.

Go forward as Light.

Danielle Olivia Mengue Me Nkoulou

ABOUT THE AUTHOR

Danielle Olivia Mengue Me Nkoulou

 is a visionary author and teacher dedicated to redefining how believers approach spiritual warfare. With a unique perspective that bridges profound biblical revelation with insights into psychology and cognitive behavior, Danielle empowers readers to move beyond a lifestyle of constant conflict into one of divine alignment and unshakable identity in Christ.

Her work emphasizes that victory is not a battle to be won, but a transformation to be experienced, becoming so full of the light of Christ that darkness has no ground. Danielle's practical teaching style, which explores concepts like the influence of spiritual choices on brain chemistry and the power of the blood covenant, provides a fresh, actionable framework for spiritual maturity.

When she isn't writing or mentoring others in their walk of faith, Danielle channels her creativity into art, which she uses as another medium to bring light and revelation to people.

You can learn more about Danielle's ministry and connect with her online at:

Lighthouseishome.com

www.ingramcontent.com/pod-product-compliance
Lightning Source LLC
Chambersburg PA
CBHW060415130626
46555CB00005B/2070